INTERDEPENDENCE IN NATURE

CONSERVATION

Endpapers: Münsterhof Square, Zurich, 1946

JOYCE JOFFE

CONSERVATION

 ALDUS BOOKS LONDON

Consultant **F. Fraser Darling,**
Vice-President of The Conservation Foundation,
Washington; Vice-President of the International
Union for the Conservation of Nature.

Series Editor	Alec Laurie
Art Director	Victor Shreeve
Designers	Brian Lee
	David Nash
Assistants	Adrian Williams
	Kevin Carver
Research	Naomi Narod
	Kate Jackson
	Judy Savage
	Michèle Rimbeaud

SBN 490 00162 9

First published in 1969 by
Aldus Books Limited
Aldus House, 17 Conway Street, London W1

© Aldus Books Limited London 1969

Printed in Italy by Arnoldo Mondadori, Verona

Contents

Pliny the Elder (A.D. 23–79) is remembered best for his Natural History *and for the way he died—observing the eruption of Vesuvius that destroyed Pompeii and Herculaneum. This picture is from a mediaeval edition of the* Natural History. *It depicts Nature as idyllic and unreal, with beasts (many of them mythical) and mankind living together in harmony and tranquility. Pliny felt otherwise: "It is far from easy to determine whether nature has proved a kind parent or a merciless step-mother".*

CHAPTER 1

HUNTERS & VISIONARIES

Almost every part of the habitable world has been influenced by man; and during his short time on earth man has wrought changes that are a monument to his ability to master his often hostile environment. Sometimes, though, he has taken the raw material of the earth and has plundered and exploited it, in ignorance and without foresight or planning.

The study of the delicate interrelationships of plants and animals, soil and climate (which together make up the environment), is the job of *ecologists*. They have only recently come to realize how fundamental a part man plays in his environment, and that any interference with it may have results that go far beyond the original change.

In this book we are going to talk about some of these results, in particular what ecologists, pedologists (soil scientists), economists, and sociologists are doing to repair some of the damage that has already been done, and to provide some sort of blueprint for preserving the earth's natural beauty and for harnessing its resources more wisely. This planning can involve the reclamation of a dust-bowl, the control of pests, the saving of a single plant or animal from extinction, the declaring of a smoke-less zone, or the development of new techniques in wheat-growing or sewage disposal. But whatever it is, it is all part of *conservation*—planning for the future.

In his earliest history, man as a hunter and food gatherer was absolutely on a par with any other animal species within the environment, except for his use of fire and tools. He had to compete with the larger carnivores for his meat, and he in his turn formed part of their diet. At first he probably avoided any direct conflict with these animals, but later, with that ingenuity so characteristic of man, he learned to trap and hunt even the most dangerous of these wild predators. Cave paintings such as those of Lascaux or Altamira depict startlingly real hunting scenes; some of these paintings could perhaps be interpreted as "wall charts" for instructing the tribe in hunting techniques. During the period of what some scientists call the "Pleistocene overkill," some 50,000 years ago, man may well have been largely responsible for the extermination of nearly half the larger African mammals—and he may have had an even more disastrous influence on North Africa, which he colonized later, about 12,000 years ago (deducible from radio-carbon dating evidence).

At this time the total human population was probably about five million, so that there was an immense amount of the earth's surface still in its natural state simply because man hadn't reached it. But about 9000 years ago, in the period known as the Neolithic Revolution, man took a great step forward that was to reduce his complete dependence on his environment: he became a farmer, and began to domesticate some of the wild beasts that he had only hunted before. For the first time he had a regular supply of meat and milk. Furthermore he used the crops he harvested in summer to feed himself in winter.

Over the next few thousand years, not only did farming and animal husbandry techniques improve, but man began to exploit the natural resources of the earth. Technology began to play an increasingly important part in the culture, and some of the settlements increased in size and became towns. This could now happen because labour could be divided among the inhabitants in such a way that not everybody was concerned with producing food. But despite the increasing use of metals and progressively sophisticated technology, man was hardly less dependent on his external environment: he was still at the mercy of drought or flood and always lived in awe and fear of unforeseen natural disaster. So at some stage he had to come to terms with his fear by learning to control and pacify the caprices of nature by offerings and gifts. This process became much elaborated into complex rituals in which he invested natural objects with personalities. The common words in the language for things like "sun" and "moon" became names.

"Sun" and "Moon" became gods. Later there were gods controlling every natural phenomenon from the care of the dead in the underworld to the annual renewal of the seasons. For example, great festivals were held in which animals and even humans were sacrificed to ensure the success of the spring crops; there was a vegetation god who died every year and rose with the spring, and to whom the farmers addressed their pleas and sacrifices.

How did all this help? It certainly did not prevent natural forces from acting. But man put them into a framework that he had made and therefore could understand. He had reduced them from forces he could not struggle against to gods he could reason with or at least bribe. By this he managed to put himself at a distance from nature; he could stand aloof from it. He could take from, use, and even despoil, nature—and nature could not touch him in the same way. It is rather frightening to realize how little our attitude has changed. In the days of Sumer, about 5000 years ago, perhaps exploitation mattered less than it does now. There were not so many people and the inroads into the natural environment were slight.

The world's population rose quite slowly; the drain on natural resources was also gradual. So until the 18th century nobody paid much attention. But around that time, the growing industrialization in Britain was causing terrible conditions and overcrowding in the cities. It was this that caught the attention of the first man to make mankind aware of an impending crisis.

Above: Ra, the Egyptian Sun god, one of the deities "responsible" for the fertility of the Nile valley. A poor crop would have been viewed as failure of the vegetation god Osiris to win the war against his brother, Set, the god of aridity and the desert. Right: The starvation that followed failure of the harvest is shown on this bas-relief from the temple of King Unis, about 2350 B.C.

The First Conservationists   In 1798, a young clergyman called Thomas Robert Malthus (1766–1834) published his *Essay on the Principle of Population*. It was he who first alerted the world to the imminent crisis by saying that human population would double each generation. This would mean a rise of population in a geometrical ratio—1, 2, 4, 8, 16, 32, 64 . . . whereas food supplies could at best increase in an arithmetical ratio—1, 2, 3, 4, 5, 6, 7. . . . Malthus's figures were somewhat exaggerated, being based on a freak population explosion in America, and his whole doctrine, as well as the remedies he proposed, was rather controversial. The main causes of the problem as he saw it were early marriage and a high birth-rate among the poor. He felt confident, however, that as living standards rose, the birth-rate would correspondingly fall. (He did not, incidentally, advocate birth-control.)

His vitriolic attacks on the poor caused a prolonged outcry; he wrote an outspoken reply to Thomas Paine's *Rights of Man* in which he denounced the Poor Laws, maintaining that public welfare and charity for the poor only made the problem worse. It provided them with money but did not increase food supplies. Prices would rise accordingly and the work-houses would become filled with increasing numbers of the "less valuable part of society" who would be totally dependent upon its "more worthy members." Needless to say, the Malthusian Doctrine, as his views were later called, was well received by the wealthy, who could now blame the misfortunes of the poor on anything but a maldistribution of wealth. Malthus is remembered today as a pioneer, and as a major influence on the thinking of Darwin and Wallace, particularly in applying the idea of population pressure to the plant and animal kingdoms; and it was partly from this idea that the concept of Natural Selection was developed. But we should like to think that Malthus's ideas about society and the value of human life are unacceptable today.

Some time later, in 1864, the American George Perkins Marsh (1801–82) published his book *Man and Nature*. Marsh, who was ambassador to Italy for 21 years, was a remarkable man with very wide interests, and he was keen on public service. He made a profound study of what he called in the book's subtitle "Physical Geography as modified by Human Action." The result of Marsh's book was that many more people began to realize that man's exploitation had often done more harm than good and that man had been heedless of the future.

Meanwhile something quite new had begun to catch the public's attention—wild life. Some people attribute this to the influence of the Romantic poets. We think particularly of Coleridge, Wordsworth, and Shelley, who did so much to alter man's accepted values about nature. Wild scenery was to be regarded no longer as "horrific"—as the British naturalist Thomas Pennant called it in 1777—but as something in which to glory. The earlier Romantics were rather more concerned with "wild thunderstorms over the lake" than with wild animals, but later, both in England and elsewhere, there were changes in this attitude.

Ninety years after Malthus attacked the Poor Laws, the Industrial Revolution had arrived. Factory workers crowded into cramped and insanitary housing. Gustav Doré's engraving gives us a realistic impression of industrial London around 1875.

This new feeling for nature caught the interest of another American, Ralph Waldo Emerson (1803–82), who travelled a great deal in Europe and was a great admirer of European culture. Emerson absorbed the new European attitude and took it back to his home town of Concord, Massachusetts, where he developed his philosophy of *transcendentalism*. We need not concern ourselves very much with this philosophy, which is so involved that one of the dictionary definitions of transcendentalism is "obscurity, incomprehensibility, and fantasy." What does matter, however, is that Emerson imported the Romantics' ideas about nature into America, and, together with the group that he assembled around him at Concord, gave them a new lease of life.

One of the members of Emerson's New England circle was a young man named Henry David Thoreau (1817–62). Today Thoreau would possibly be regarded as something of a "drop-out," who had chosen to avoid the hard facts of earning a living because he questioned whether there was any virtue in work for its own sake. He suggested, for example, that the order of the week should be reversed so that only one day was set aside for work, leaving the remainder for enjoyment of leisure activities. The way to such enjoyment, he considered, was through greater understanding both of the inner self and of the outer environment of nature. Emerson lent him a few acres of land around Walden Pond, near Concord, and he lived there alone for two years. He did not completely renounce civilization for the hermit's life; but he revelled in his intimate communion with nature. In an age of growing

Left: An arcadian landscape by Claude Lorrain (1600–1682) of Aeneas at Delos, in which Nature is depicted as static and unreal.

Right: The full fury of Nature and of Man's involvement in it, can be seen in this painting by J. M. W. Turner, who lived from 1775–1851, about the time of the beginning of the Romantic Movement.

materialism he saw the natural environment as an outlet, an "open end" to civilization, that could help men to fulfil themselves and to understand their own potential. He wrote several essays and books recording his experiences at Walden Pond as well as his observations on nature and the uses to which man put it in many parts of the North American continent. Most of his books, such as *Walden*, or *Life in the Woods*, and *A Week on the Concord*, are thus an odd mixture of autobiographical detail, philosophy, and natural history.

You may well be wondering at this point how Thoreau can be linked with conservation. The answer is that among the survey party that first penetrated into the Yellowstone country (of Wyoming and Montana) in 1868–9 there were four young men who talked around a camp fire one night and conceived there the idea of setting the Yellowstone aside as a permanent preserve. Three of these men came from New England, and all four had certainly read and been influenced by Thoreau. As a result of their enthusiasm, this great area was declared a national park in 1872.

In those early years, national parks were not as we know them today. They were tracts of land set aside mainly for sport. No permanent settlement was permitted—only camping; but one could hunt and fish quite freely.

Around the turn of the century, however, the herds of wild deer and buffalo that had once been so numerous began to disappear from their native prairie. Both had been a mainstay of Indians and settlers. The buffalo especially had been slaughtered without control during the 19th century by

professional hunters who followed the railway construction gangs out west. They ran a lucrative business until the decline in game made it unprofitable.

Theodore Roosevelt, who was president during this critical period, realized that the game needed some protection. He was a fairly keen big-game hunter himself, so his motives were hardly altruistic. However he was far-sighted enough to practice restraint. It was he who coined the phrase "Never shoot a doe." This worked very well just after the felling of the great forests of America, when there was an enormous amount of secondary growth of vegetation and small trees. Indeed it worked too well. Today there are still plenty of sportsmen in the United States, and a great annual kill of deer, but the notion of never shooting a doe took such a firm hold that there are now far too many deer in some places: for example, the householders of Montclair in New Jersey have to spray their shrubs with a compound that discourages the deer from eating them.

During the same period, other countries were following in America's wake with plans of their own. As early as 1889, Britain had founded the Royal Society for the Protection of Birds, followed six years later by the National Trust. But strangely enough, for a country so well endowed with enthusiastic amateur naturalists, Britain has had a very poor record until fairly recently. The Fauna Preservation Society was formed in 1903, but it was then often called a "society of retired butchers." The people who formed the nucleus of this society were also sportsmen—many of them army officers who took their leave in places such as Kashmir or Kenya, where there were plenty of animals to shoot. Inevitably, these animals too began to decline in numbers. As with the Americans, the members of the society began to plan to conserve their game stocks. But although animal conservation began in this way, there was a gradual change in attitude toward conservation for its own sake. It is interesting to trace this change in the career of one of these big-game hunters, Col. Richard Meinertzhagen. When he was in Kenya in 1904 he would go out and shoot three rhinoceros before lunch. In his *Kenya Diary* he admits to having been obsessed by an unashamed blood lust. "Hunting," he says, "is man's primitive instinct, and I indulged in it and enjoyed it to the full." He justified his actions to some extent by remarking that more than three quarters of the animals he shot went to provide much-needed meat for his African troops. Thirty years later, however, his attitude had changed and he became a member of the Fauna Preservation Society and until his death in 1967 he was on the side of the conservationists.

As we have seen, an attitude of restraint toward wild life has been steadily growing this century. But this regard for living things, not for food but for their intrinsic value, could not have become practicable until man had become sufficiently independent of wild animals as a danger to himself. Nor perhaps could it have happened without the aid of films and television.

Enthusiasm for the wild beast, safely behind bars in a zoo or on film, is certainly a product of the affluent society. (Indians do not have warm feelings for a man-eating tiger.) This enthusiasm is genuine but all too often it is

The Romantic Movement, which spread from
Europe, was characterized by a change from
utilitarian to aesthetic standards in the Arts
generally. Henry David Thoreau (1817–1862),
was one of the purists of literary romanticism in
America.

uncritical and ill-informed. It has an aspect that could be called a "Bambi complex"—the cooing, sentimental regard for individual animals that, at its worst, results in gushing over puppies and young polar bears. Walt Disney was perhaps the first person to bring animals to the attention of a wide public. He can perhaps be held partly responsible for the "Bambi complex," which gets its name from one of his first cartoon films about animals. But although these cartoons tended to be crushingly sentimental, his nature films such as *The Living Desert* and *The Vanishing Prairie* are excellent and true to life. They portrayed the ugliness as well as the beauty and they captured the public imagination as nothing had done before.

Since then there has been a considerable increase in animal and zoo films, mostly for television. These films do admirable work, by bringing the animal world into our homes; they have very enthusiastic audiences, and not only among the young. They are doing a lot toward broadening the public's outlook. There are still instances of the old sentimental attitude, however, such as came to light at the wrecking of the *Torrey Canyon* in 1967. There was a world-wide outcry when this giant oil tanker split open on the Seven Stones Reef, off Cornwall, spilling out some 100,000 tons of oil to spoil beaches and rocks and kill many thousands of sea birds. People who had never seen a razorbill or a guillemot were stunned that so many of these birds should be killed needlessly when they were on their way to their breeding grounds.

One of the aims of conservation is to prevent this sort of thing from happening, if possible. But is it the only, or even the principal, aim? While conservationists in the more highly industrialized countries are concerning themselves with the preservation of wild life, areas for research, or space for recreation, people in other, less fortunate, countries are concerned with a more urgent problem. In a number of these countries farmland has been grossly overworked and is becoming less and less useful for growing crops and grazing animals. Even prosperous America suffered this in the 1930s when exploitation of the corn-growing lands reduced many areas to a dust-bowl. Prompt action, and new techniques such as contour ploughing, soon restored the land to a useful condition; but many countries have not been so fortunate. They lack America's capital and agricultural know-how, and most of them have to contend with overcrowding, poverty, and terrible food shortage. Later in this book we shall be talking more about these problems and about how they affect every one of us.

At the beginning of this chapter we talked about ecologists, and how their job is so necessary in planning for conservation. In this book we shall see many examples of ecologists at work, but first we must step aside to take a look at the basic facts of ecology itself and to get acquainted with the rules that govern the natural order of living things.

Above: One of the most unspoiled parts of England; Tarn Hows in the Lake District. The whole area is popular for walking, climbing and simply for "getting back to nature." Below: The hunger for greenery is shown in the rather sad picture of a garden on a rooftop in Central London; the lawn is made of plastic.

Life began in the sea and some living things (such as the dolphin) returned to the sea after a long period of their evolution had been spent on land. In nature, animals, plants, land, and water all form part of a complex and ever-changing network.

22

CHAPTER 2

A.B.C. OF ECOLOGY

Every boy or girl who has watched tadpoles grow into frogs in a jam jar or grown beans in damp cotton wool has learnt a little bit about ecology; so has anyone who has ever been fishing, or gone for a picnic in the woods. Learning ecology is basically a matter of observation; it is amazing what we can learn simply by keeping our eyes open. But this is not really enough; we need some framework into which to fit our observations. In the same way, since this book applies ecology to conservation, we cannot go far without first understanding the basic principles.

Ecology is mainly about animal and plant populations in their natural environment. Its aim is to study the natural laws that control living things, and eventually to build up as complete a picture as possible by collecting detailed information from all over the world. The whole world is, in a sense, an environment. But it is too unwieldy to study as a whole; it would take several lifetimes to understand it in any detail. Ecologists therefore usually study a small area at a time. How small is small? Some ecologists study the organisms living in a thimbleful of soil; others study larger units, such as a forest or a mountain range, but they use very similar methods because all environments have certain things in common. The purpose of studying them is to establish the principles that govern living things in the environment— what ecologists call *living systems*. All living systems need an energy supply, and they get it from the sun. The sun's energy is used to make food and this food is used and re-used in a *cycle* that we shall now describe.

Primary Producers   All animal life depends, directly or indirectly, on green plants. The reason is that only plants are able to make their own food and store it in the form of sugar and starch—animals cannot. To do this plants use nothing but water and carbon dioxide, with sunlight to supply energy, and a pigment called *chlorophyll*, which causes the green colour of leaves. The process is called *photosynthesis*. Only plants containing chlorophyll can photosynthesize; but not all plants are green. There are many plants that also contain other chlorophyll-like substances of different colours (carotin or xanthophyll); and these mask the familiar green colour.

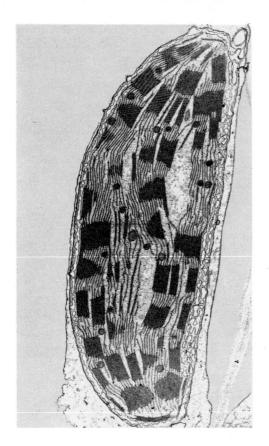

*Above: A chloroplast magnified
27,000 times. Photosynthesis,
the complex process by which
the sun's energy is converted
into chemical energy (sugar) is
carried out here. Below:
Chlorophyll (contained in the
chloroplasts) absorbs more light
from the red and blue-green
wave-lengths than from the rest
of the sun's spectrum for
photosynthesis. Right: The
process in action at various
levels in a forest.*

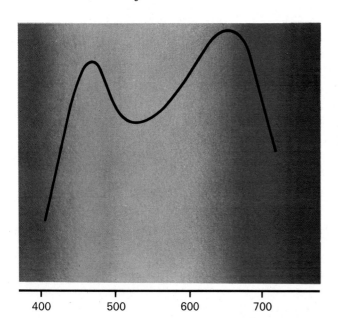

400   500   600   700

Because plants occupy the fundamental position in living systems, ecologists call them the *primary producers*. Not only do they manufacture food for animals; they also have other functions. For example, plants provide a cover for bare earth and their roots bind the topsoil, so that it cannot be blown or washed away. The remains of decayed plants, as we shall see, make up a vital constituent of all healthy soils.

Consumers All living things except green plants are *consumers*. This means that they do not manufacture food themselves but must get it from the producers, either directly or indirectly. The consumers include all animals, and also certain plants, such as fungi, that do not contain chlorophyll. (Fungi cannot photosynthesize, and, like animals, they live by drawing nourishment from other living or dead plants or animals.)

Animals fall into two groups—the plant-eaters (*herbivores*), such as dugongs, sheep, and cattle, and the meat-eaters (*carnivores*), such as sharks, lions, and wolves. (Carnivores prey on other animals so they are often called *predators*.) Thus the cycle in each living system is like a circular chain made up of several links. The first link consists of plants; the second, of herbivores, or *primary consumers*; the third, of carnivores, or *secondary consumers*. There can be *tertiary consumers*, too—one carnivore often eats another, usually smaller, carnivore.

When any animal dies or is killed and partly eaten by a carnivore, scavengers and carrion feeders move in. These might be vultures or hyenas, but they could also be beetles or millipedes that feed on dead flesh. Meanwhile, bacteria also invade the carcass and eat what is left. Bacterial action breaks down the complex molecules of muscle and bone; sooner or later, depending on the climate, the carcass will have completely disappeared, having been carried away or broken down into simple chemical compounds such as nitrates, phosphates, carbon dioxide, and water. It has been said that if there were no bacteria that could digest and break down *chitin* (the horny material of insects' skeletons) the entire world would be buried in cast-off insect corpses.

Clearly the job that scavengers and bacteria do is the vital one of returning nutrients to the soil and air for re-use. Their contribution almost completes the cycle, and the simple chemical compounds can be taken in through the plant roots and supply the shoots and leaves with everything they need.

To complete the picture we must now see what happens to the plants. If plants die without being eaten, they fall to the ground and are quickly broken down into simpler compounds. Water is one of the main agents, together with a weak acid called *humic acid*. Bacterial action also plays its role in converting part of the dead and decaying plants, together with animal remains and excreta, into moist brown *humus*. It is impossible to exaggerate the importance of humus; it is an essential part of soil. Soil in fact consists of particles of rock surrounded by this spongy material, which is a complex mixture of living and dead matter. It provides a store-house of nutrients

Plant matter is the first link in the food chain. The second link is the primary consumer (herbivore) represented here by a zebra. The efficiency of conversion of vegetation into zebra meat is only about 10 per cent; the remainder is lost as heat.

27

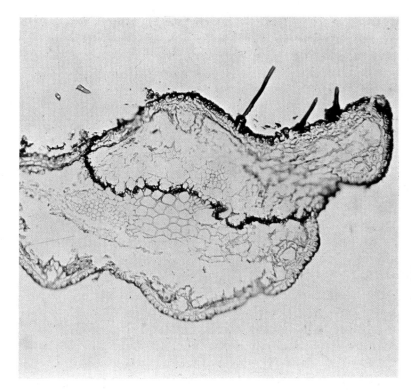

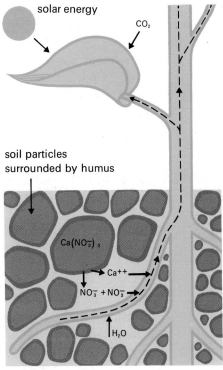

solar energy

CO_2

soil particles
surrounded by humus

$Ca(NO_3^-)_2$

Ca^{++}

$NO_3^- + NO_3^-$

H_2O

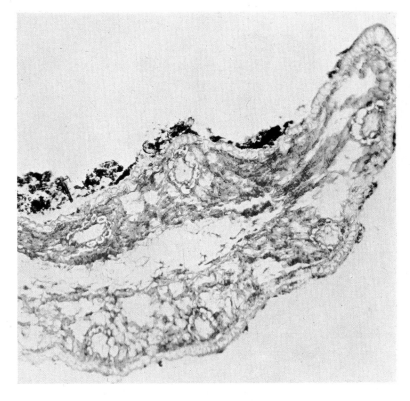

*Opposite: Third link in the
food chain; a buzzard,
carnivorous predator, kills and
eats a herbivorous rabbit. Small
scavengers will dispose of the
remains.*

*Top left: Cross section
showing pine needle being
penetrated by fungus (black).
Mites have begun to eat the
centre; decay has begun.*

*Below left: Later stage in
decay of pine needle. Both
centre and fungus are now
almost eaten away by mites
and worms whose droppings
appear (black) on concave side.*

*Above: Final stage in food
chain. Breakdown products from
humus surrounding rock
particles. Humus retains final
results of decomposition as
inorganic salts; these ionize in
soil water and return to the
plant primary producer via its
roots.*

that plants need in order to grow, and also makes it possible for plant roots to breathe, for roots need oxygen. It also makes plant growth possible in different kinds of soil. A clay soil, for instance, consists of extremely small particles of rock surrounded by humus; if there is insufficient humus, the particles pack together so tightly that the clay gets waterlogged, and plant roots die from lack of oxygen. The same soil, if it dries out, becomes as hard as a brick, so again the roots are strangled and can neither breathe nor force their way through the soil. At the opposite end of the scale, a sandy soil consists of much coarser particles, through which rain-water can percolate very quickly, washing down any nutrient salts—a process called *leaching*—and leaving the topsoil dry. Here again a good supply of humus is essential in order to keep salts, water, and oxygen in contact with the roots.

Food Chains and Webs   All the organic and inorganic material in the system is recycled in the so-called *food chain*. Only the energy supply fed in by photosynthesis seeps inexorably away at each stage in the chain.

A food chain can consist of five links: for example, grass—antelope—lion—beetle—bacteria. Although we can write this down as a simple series, such simplicity seldom occurs in nature. Every living thing is potentially part of several other possible food chains—the antelope might be eaten by a lion or a leopard, and the grass it feeds on could be the food of hippos, wildebeeste, and many other grazers. Also, the lion itself may eat several types of animals, both carnivores and herbivores. Large numbers of food chains thus link with

All that can be seen of a living ecosystem here is its external appearance; the rest is seen only after careful observation and study. Left: An ecosystem under the sea, the Great Barrier Reef, off Queensland. Right: High in the Ruwenzori Mountains of the Congo, where the vegetation just below the snow line consists mainly of tree groundsels.

one another in a wide variety of ways, and the result is a sort of multi-dimensional food chain known as a *food web*. When an ecologist tries to unravel a food web his difficulties really begin: the permutations seem endless. Also, the boundaries of the food web are never clear; they tend to merge and interact with the neighbouring food webs all around. For the purpose of studying one in isolation, however, we have to draw a line, and consider, if possible, the interrelationships of every living thing within a limited area.

Ecosystems Nothing exists in isolation and every living thing is affected not only by its neighbours, but by its non-living surroundings too. Thus no ecological study is complete if it leaves out such things as soil, wind, light intensity, temperature, humidity, and so on. The whole living system, including these non-living factors, makes up an *ecosystem*.

Although we study an ecosystem as if it were a fairly stable unit, it is actually a very complex and dynamic structure. The appearance of an unchanging equilibrium is only superficial. Why is everything constantly changing? The short answer is that an ecosystem is usually packed to capacity with plants and animals. But at any given time, depending on the particular ecosystem, there will almost certainly be a shortage of something—food, space, or water, for instance. Whenever a shortage occurs, competition increases; when there is a surplus, competition declines. Overabundance may result in a population rise, which in turn causes a food or space shortage, and so competition again becomes intense.

Adaptability Every living thing struggles to survive. Plants, for example, compete constantly for sunlight and nutrients. If one ground-dwelling plant happens to produce a variant that can cling to the bark of a tree, and if successive offspring of that variant retain this characteristic, then eventually a climber will evolve. By climbing, that plant raises itself to a position where there is far less competition for sunlight, and so it improves its chances of survival. Take another example, this time concerning animals. In some regions animals compete fiercely for every blade of grass. So an animal that is a grass-eater will become slightly better off if it can also live on other vegetation—say, dandelions. If it succeeds in adapting itself to this new food it will side-step competition; but it can do this in more than one way. It might, for instance, discover a preference for dandelions and continue to eat only dandelions; or alternatively it might become more versatile and even eat shoots of young trees. Both these examples show us how a living thing becomes adapted to its surroundings; however, the first becomes specialized while the second becomes unspecialized but remains versatile. An animal that takes up a particular diet and way of life may well find that it has few or no rivals. But the disadvantage of this is that it may become so conservative (like the anteater, which has become adapted to a diet of ants) that if the surrounding conditions change it will not be able to alter its habits. Survival so often depends on just this quality of adaptability, that the specialized animal is usually a short-lived species by the standards of the geological time scale. There are certain animals and plants (so-called "living fossils") that have stayed much the same for millions of years, but this is because they have become adapted to an environment that is itself particularly unchanging.

Adaptability, then, is useful in a fast-changing ecosystem, but it is not something you can see in action. A casual look at an ecosystem will not reveal the constant fierce competition of its inhabitants; at any single moment each creature usually appears to be adapted for its way of life—it fits, so to speak, into a hole in the ecosystem known as its *ecological niche*.

Some ecosystems contain far more ecological niches than others. This becomes obvious when you compare, say, the antarctic ice-cap with a tropical forest. Clearly, there can be only a limited number of living things able to survive six months of intense cold and very little daylight, as well as a ground cover of permanent snow. Certainly, there is only one species of animal that does this—the emperor penguin. A tropical forest, on the other hand, is teeming with plant and animal life; it offers far more possible niches than an ice-cap. An ecological niche can be named after the diet of its occupant: a carnivore such as a lion occupies a general "carnivore" niche. There can also be very specialized niches: a good example is Darwin's finches of the Galapagos Islands.

Scavengers occupy ecological niches too, and so do soil bacteria and trees, parasites and fungi. The great diversity of living things today is the direct and indirect result of countless attempts by living things to stay put in their ecological niches over the millions of years of changing conditions.

Epiphytes such as these tropical club-mosses and ferns have abandoned the soil in favour of a place nearer the sunlight. They anchor their roots in crevices in trees and derive nourishment from humus that collects in them and from the rain.

Natural Selection   We have talked so far about the forms of life that exist within an ecosystem; but we have not yet described how the system operates. What are the natural forces that have produced the great variety of living things? What is the result of competition between living things?

The most important single answer was put forward in 1858 by two Englishmen, Charles Darwin and Alfred Russel Wallace. These two naturalists were the first to recognize the meaning of the constant battle in nature. It was they who realized that it was nature's way of keeping numbers approximately constant in any given ecosystem. They saw also that in the struggle for survival the survivors were successful because they were in some way "better fitted" than their unsuccessful rivals, and this observation led to Darwin's well-known phrase—"survival of the fittest." But what does "fitness" mean? Basically, fitness is a general term describing the quality that allows one individual to survive long enough to breed at the expense of another—even its own sibling. It may be a question of speed, camouflage, temperature tolerance, or faster breeding cycle, depending on the quality necessary at the time. The individual that has the quality that saves its life possesses it almost invariably by chance. Often such a quality is the result of a lucky combination of genes inherited from its parents. There are also genetical "mistakes" called *mutations*, which occur naturally and may alter the genes in an unexpected and occasionally favourable way. Also an element of pure luck may be the decisive factor during the life of the individual and cannot be discounted. Even genetically identical twins do not have absolutely identical experiences during their lives, and any slight difference may determine which of the two survives.

The greater the shortages of food or space the greater will be the so-called "selection pressure," to weed out the less fit individuals *before* they have reached maturity. If they survive to produce another generation, the young will be just as ill adapted. Thus it is often a matter of luck if a variation of plant or animal is favourable enough to be refined by trial and error so that it can *breed true*—that is, continue in the same new way in following generations. This process, which is in fact *evolution*, usually takes a very long time in nature; life on earth has been evolving for at least 1000 million years. Horticulturalists and animal-breeders, however, can breed several new varieties of plants and animals in a single human lifetime by intensive *artificial* selection. They do this by preventing unfavourable mutations from breeding, and selecting only favourable mutations and other desirable characteristics. Although this is not natural, it is an excellent method of studying the evidence for evolution and understanding its mechanisms.

Growth of Ecosystems   So far we have talked of ecosystems as being, to some extent, stable and unchanging. But this kind of stability occurs only in an ecosystem that has developed as far as it can go. For example, the mature forest is a stable ecosystem; if it is not interfered with, it will last for thousands of years. And when we talk about interference, we mean anything from a major change of climate to an accidental fire started by a cigarette.

But if we think back to the early history of our planet, when the earth was too hot to support life, and when there was no soil at all, only bare rock, we can see that such a forest could not have sprung up ready-made with all its plant and animal inhabitants. The best way to show what we mean is to trace briefly the history of a section of land from the time when it was barren rock, perhaps newly raised up out of the sea or lava spewed up by a volcano that gradually cooled and solidified.

Successions The rock is lifeless, but it is exposed to air and to the action of rain, wind, sun, and frost. Alternate heating and cooling causes cracks to form in the rock. The rain, with its content of dilute carbonic acid, begins to dissolve out some of the minerals. The surface begins to weather, and small rock particles collect in the crevices.

The first living things to establish themselves on the bare rocky slopes are *lichens*. These consist of a fungus and an alga (another simple plant) living in association as one plant. The wind carries their spores to the rock, where they gain a foothold; and as the lichen grows it gradually penetrates the cracks, dissolves a bit more of the rock, and uses the dissolved salts for nutrients. This first stage can take a long time to get established—perhaps many years. Gradually, as each lichen dies, its remains decay and leave small quantities of humus. The rock dust and the humus very slowly build up into a thin layer of soil that provides a suitable home for small organisms such as mites, spiders, and ants. This combination of plants and animals is known as the *pioneer community*; it is composed only of organisms that can withstand very tough conditions. As soon as a thriving pioneer community is established and a greater thickness of soil is built up, mosses and other small plants move in, followed by worms, bacteria, moulds, and, still later, grass. Grass also has an important mechanical function: because it grows taller than any of its predecessors in the succession, it provides cover and shade; and if it is high and dense it acts as a wind-break that prevents water from evaporating. Other plants that need shade and moisture, such as shrubs, can then grow. Finally, tree seeds are able to take root; after trees begin to grow, one species is displaced by another until a permanent forest develops. Thus, in this example the stages in the succession are: heath-land—scrub—open wood-land—dense forest. This is called the *primary succession*. But it is only a single example and does not suggest that in every succession the final stage is the development of a forest; tundra vegetation (lichens and small willows) is the final stage for arctic conditions. When it is reached, however, it will be self-perpetuating and stable. It is then called a *climax*. Each earlier stage destroys itself by providing the conditions for the following stage to establish itself. But the climax is stable; if undisturbed it can, in theory, continue indefinitely.

Any stage in the succession may be suspended and prevented from following its natural course. Floods, fires, and hurricanes may cause a temporary set-back of varying severity, or the natural balance of grazing and browsing animals may prevent the development of climax vegetation more or less indefinitely. Man has been able to use the natural succession for his own advantage by deliberately cutting back forest for agricultural land or pasture. When destruction causes only a temporary set-back, succession is resumed; and this will usually follow the original pattern closely (except, for example, when destruction is due to atomic radiation). Normally a so-called *secondary succession* grows up that, in its final stages at least, could be indistinguishable from the primary succession. A succession may take anything from a human lifetime to a thousand years to reach a climax. Strangely enough these rules usually apply only to land succession. In the sea there is no true succession, as

Left: The new volcanic island of Surtsey, near Iceland provides ideal experimental conditions for studying the build-up of a succession from the very beginning. Pioneer communities become established on existing rocks such as the granite shown below, where lichens and some mosses have gained a hold in the rock. It depends upon the type of rock and on the climate and altitude what type of succession develops. It may be that only lichens and mosses can survive on this exposed and steep mountainous slope. Opposite: A final stage in the development of a succession; in this particular region, the climax is a forest with Douglas fir. It is stable and self-perpetuating.

no community influences the environment enough to create a stable climax.

In certain environments, especially in the temperate and colder zones, the climax vegetation will consist of only a few types of plants, and we tend to name the climax after the most abundant that occur. For example, we may refer to "coniferous forest" or "oak-hickory forest." But in the tropics, the ecosystem is made up of so many different types of plants and animals that we cannot single out a predominant one to typify the climax.

Stratification   A climax forest is divided into layers, each with its own particular grouping of animals; and an animal will often spend its entire life

within a single layer. Some kinds of monkeys and birds, for instance, live only in the tops of the high trees, in what is called the *canopy*. Others keep to the middle branches, preferring more shade. On the ground lives a huge variety of animals, ranging from grazing mammals and carnivores to beetles and worms. Every member of this stratified society is adapted for one sort of ecological niche and no other.

As we know, a habitat is unstable unless it forms part of a climax. What, then, happens to the animal and plant populations that were part of the earlier (*subclimax*) stages of succession? The short answer is that as an area develops toward a climax vegetation, the plants and animals that lived in the subclimax stages either die off and become extinct in that area, or move on in order to keep pace with the advancing edge of the ecosystem.

Fluctuation   In any ecosystem there are fluctuations in the populations of animals and plants. There are times when the weather favours the growth of a particular plant, and this is directly reflected in the number of animals feeding on that plant. The effect is much quicker if these herbivores have a short life-cycle; for instance, the number of caterpillars that feed on the spring leaves of an oak-tree is far greater if the spring is dry and warm; so there should be a larger crop of butterflies. Conversely, a cold wet spring kills off a large number of caterpillars, and the butterfly population is reduced. This variation in population is called *fluctuation*, and the example we have just given is one of the simplest forms—depending only on weather.

We can, however, carry the story a stage further. If we assume a large caterpillar population we can also say that the other animals that are predators on caterpillars will also prosper. For instance, one predator is the ichneumon fly, which lays its eggs in caterpillars. The eggs hatch into larvae and when fully developed they eat their way out, after first consuming the still-living caterpillar's flesh. A plentiful supply of fat caterpillars thus leads to an increase in ichneumon fly population, but the caterpillars die and there is a corresponding reduction in the next generation of butterflies.

Other and slower forms of fluctuation exist among mammals and their predators, but the picture is not nearly as straightforward as it is with the insects. There are other factors besides simple supply and demand, as we shall see in Chapter 7, when we discuss population pressures.

We have touched on food chains and food webs, ecosystems, natural selection, succession, stratification, and fluctuation. These are the basics of ecology. So far, in order to keep the ecological picture as simple as possible, we have not included man; however, in the next chapter we discuss man's place in nature.

Above right: The doe and her twin fawns show well the way in which equilibrium is preserved in nature. Twins are born only in a year when food is plentiful. If food is scarce, deer may have single fawns or may not breed at all.
Below: Despite these natural fertility controls, fluctuations in population occur, and evidently there are more deer than there is food in this forest. Needing about six pounds of food per day, deer have eaten all the twigs and leaves in reach.

This mediaeval idea of the Earth with Jerusalem at its centre, has given place to more realistic views as our knowledge of geography has increased. But changes in ideas do not come easily; we are loath to revise our beliefs. This chapter is designed to stir up some healthy controversy about a few of our dearly held values; a familiar world seen from a slightly different angle. If we pose a few questions you may not have asked yourself before, so much the better.

CHAPTER 3

PUTTING MAN IN PERSPECTIVE

Whenever a really new and revolutionary contribution to scientific thought is made, we are thrown into confusion. All too often the greatest thinkers and innovators have been denounced as heretics and have had to pay dearly for disturbing the equilibrium, especially when the weight of their evidence was so convincing that it became ludicrous to go on thinking in the old ways. Galileo Galilei (1564–1642), for instance, made many discoveries in the fields of mathematics and astronomy; and he was the first to prove that the earth goes round the sun. Far from welcoming this astonishing new discovery, the Catholic Church forced Galileo to recant and he spent his last eight years under house arrest. Since then we have learnt much more about astronomy, and consequently about the earth; we now know that the earth is a small planet revolving round a rather insignificant star (the sun) somewhere on one of the outer arms of a spiral nebula (our own galaxy, which we see end-on as the Milky Way). But today, more than three centuries later, our way of life is still based on the idea that the earth has a special place in the universe.

Let us look at another major breakthrough—Darwin's book *The Origin of Species* (1859). In this book Darwin produced a great mass of evidence to show that new species are constantly evolving, and he completely exploded the accepted doctrine that each living thing was created separately. But new ways of thinking are never easy to accept. Darwin himself admitted that coming to terms with this idea of his was "like confessing a murder." Inevitably the book started controversy, but his later work, *The Descent of Man* (1871), caused an even greater uproar; people could not, or would not, see themselves as descended from ape-like ancestors. But today Darwin's theories about evolution (together with the later discoveries about the actual mechanism of inheritance by genes) are the foundations on which biological classification is based. And yet there are still places in the United States where it is illegal to teach evolution in schools. Even those of us who are familiar with evolutionary concepts still do not see ourselves as close cousins of the chimpanzee.

At first, Darwin's ideas had very little impact. Even George Perkins Marsh (p. 14), who was a contemporary of Darwin, was entirely uninfluenced by arguments about evolution that were raging at the time (though it is possible that he had not read *The Origin of Species*). Marsh's ideas about conservation were startling and new, but there was nothing new in his ideas about the nature of man. In the preface to his book *Man and Nature* (1864) he says: "The purpose of this book is . . . to illustrate the doctrine that man is, in both kind and degree, a power of a higher order than any of the other forms of animated life. . . ." Although the American and European public for whom Marsh was writing was being bombarded with new ideas about evolution, it still largely held fast to its conviction about the uniqueness of man. And even after a century of Darwinism we are, characteristically, still convinced not only that we are unique, but that we are here to stay.

We have not got ourselves into perspective. Speculations about our future evolution tend to be rather horrific: for example, a race of men with tiny legs (through lack of use) and enormous heads. Similarly, when we talk about our past evolution our remarks are often accompanied by ape-like movements, as if to emphasize how different we are now. Science fiction is crammed with weird space creatures with scales and television aerials sticking out of their heads, but have you noticed that at least they usually have heads, and something like bodies, arms, and legs? The belief that extraterrestrial monsters are basically rather like us is called *anthropomorphism*—(from the Greek *anthropos*, man, and *morphe*, form). We are often anthropomorphic in our attitudes to animals too: "He understands every word I say!" But, as we shall see, the truth is rather different.

Only the Latest Model By definition, the practice of conservation requires that one species assume responsibility for the entire earth and all other species. This single species manipulates the earth, its natural resources, and living things according to a long-term plan based mainly on ecological principles plus economics. This plan, however, has not yet been properly worked out and is full of conflicts of priorities and of economic interests—both private and national. The conventional view is that we, as a species, should assume this burden of responsibility. But we are only the latest kind of advanced vertebrate to gain a major ecological foothold; we are not necessarily the ultimate form of life on this planet. By intending to put this long-term plan of conservation into practice, we are taking for granted, firstly, that we occupy a *unique ecological position*, and, secondly, that we have the *authority*. Have we the right to do this? Should we feel responsible for the earth? These are some of the questions we shall be discussing in this chapter.

Sophisticated Apes When Perkins Marsh said that we are "a power of a higher order," he was in effect saying that the differences we perceive between ourselves and all other species are differences not only in *degree* but in *kind* as well. Can we still accept this today?

Let us examine some of the evidence. If our uniqueness is in question, our authority must be in question too. We can safely say that no animal living

Created in our own image: Left, a cyberman from
B.B.C. science fiction serial Dr. Who. Right:
The mandrake, a plant with narcotic properties,
but because men thought that its forked roots
resembled a man, they endowed it with magical
properties and believed that it cried out when
pulled from the ground. Below: Advertisement
for dog food. Dogs have a human image, and
vice versa.

today can rival us in intelligence. We have used this intelligence to develop a very sophisticated way of expressing abstract ideas by speech and writing; and we have also developed a technology far in advance of any other living thing on this planet. It would therefore be pointless to question our intellectual *superiority*. But superiority is by definition a question of degree and not of kind.

How far has our behaviour really advanced from that of our immediate primate ancestors? *The Naked Ape*, a recent book by the English zoologist Desmond Morris, is most enlightening on this subject. We have known for some time that in certain ways our physical make-up is like that of an ape: for example, there is a similar distribution of body hair on ourselves and on an embryo (not an adult) ape—hence the title, *The Naked Ape*. But the similarities go deeper than mere appearances—after all, our basic needs are the same as those of other animals. We are driven by the same needs for food, for sex, and for mastery over territory, and to satisfy them we are capable of killing both other animals and each other. Many other animals often fight fiercely (but rarely to the death) among themselves; stags do it very dramatically, when they are fighting for possession of a harem of does. They can also put on a very convincing display of aggression, in order to establish territorial rights over a particular piece of ground, or higher prestige in the community. Incidentally, apart from fighting, many animals have other interesting ways of defining their territory; for instance, hippos defecate and dogs urinate at intervals around the margins of their chosen areas—if you have a dog you must have noticed this when you take it for a walk. When we plant flags, build walls and fences, and demarcate political boundaries, we are also exhibiting territorial behaviour.

But what of the characteristics that we think of more as "human": tenderness and co-operation, for example? Desmond Morris gives this instance of true co-operation between two chimpanzees: "A female chimpanzee with a small cinder in her left eye was seen to approach a male, whimpering and obviously in distress. The male sat down and examined her intently and then proceeded to remove the cinder with great care and precision, gently using the tips of one finger from each hand."

Scientists are becoming increasingly aware that, in our behaviour at least, we are not different in kind from other advanced apes. But what the scientists say and what the public accepts are, as we know, very different.

Anyway, before we can accept—even in theory—the concept that we are just advanced apes, we need more evidence from other fields. What about our influence on our surroundings?

Man-made Environment Every living thing influences its surroundings to some extent. Every plant and animal contributes something to the dynamic equilibrium of its ecosystem and helps to perpetuate it and keep it stable. The conventional view is, however, that we as a species make a different kind of contribution to our surroundings—a contribution that is not natural, but

*One of the more conspicuous
features of behaviour common to
man and other animals is
yawning, an involuntary
response to boredom or lack
of oxygen*

45

artificial. We have modified our surroundings; we have covered much of the earth with concrete and converted the primeval forest into cornfields and even deserts.

However, if we believe that man is an animal, we can make no distinction between natural and artificial; the conventional view, which maintains that our environment is artificial simply because it is man-made, cannot be acceptable to us. Why is a skyscraper made of steel and concrete artificial because it is man-made, and a termites' nest made of mud natural because it is termite-made? The idea of something being artificial because it is made by one species and natural because it is made by another is plainly illogical. If we are animals, then *our* environment is natural too. We can alter it, but the alterations will still be natural because we, like any other animal, are a part of our ecosystem. We know that we are not the first species to achieve dominance, and in time we shall probably be replaced by a more successful form of life. In the past, other animals have made similar impacts on the

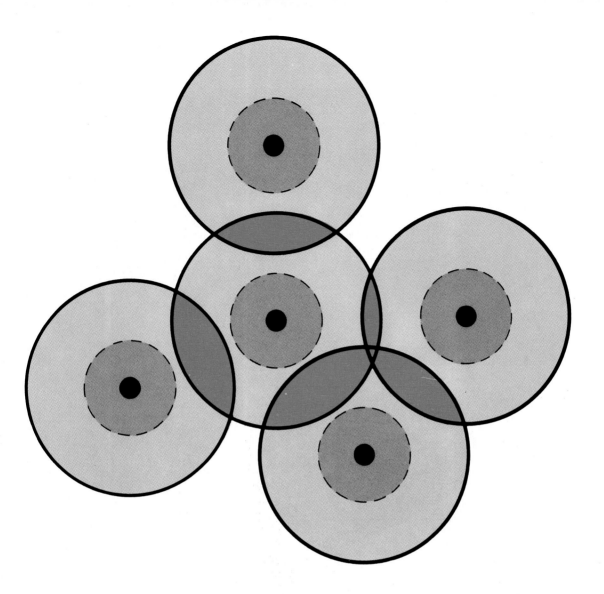

The importance of territory:
Left: A village in Kisumu,
Kenya. A fence surrounds the
village and the cattle compound
is its centre. Above: Diagram
of territoriality in birds. The
black spots are the nesting sites,
the light green represents the
food gathering areas. These
may overlap, but not the
highly defended territories shown
in grey. Below: A male sage
grouse adopting a threatening
posture in defence of its
nesting ground.

Closely packed hexagons make a strong, stable framework for building and for dividing space economically. Wasps (left) and man (right) are among the animals that have adapted the hexagon for their particular needs.

environment; let us take the example of the dinosaurs. During their hundred million years of dominance there were few ecosystems that they or their close relatives did not influence. They reached their position by competing in the struggle for survival and winning, and the inevitable by-product was the extinction of a large number of less well adapted species. We, too, have caused several extinctions in our own species' rise to dominance. The question is, why is our own ecological success considered as different from that of the dinosaurs?

"Extinction" or "Extermination" One of the things that disturb conservationists about our own dominance on earth is that many other species have, apparently, been killed off as a direct result of our success. The conventional view is clearly stated by the Swiss ecologist Vinzenz Ziswiler in his book called *Extinct and Vanishing Animals* (1967): "There are, however, essential, significant differences between the natural extinction of individual species and the extermination caused by man. Species dying a natural evolutionary death are almost always replaced by new forms or entire new groups of forms, which in turn bud, flourish, and blossom. When a species receives its death sentence through other than natural means, no new form appears in its place. Thus every species that is exterminated or killed off represents an absolute loss."

Let us examine what he says. First, "a natural evolutionary death" is not something laid down in a book of rules. The life expectancy of different species varies a tremendous amount: some species remain adapted to their surroundings and last a long time; others become extinct relatively quickly, perhaps because they have failed to cope with changing conditions. (The probable life expectancy of a species can be predicted by statistical methods, but statistics are meant to give only a very general guide line.) Then, Ziswiler assumes that, in nature, replacement by new forms nearly always occurs if species become extinct; but that if an animal has been wiped out by "other than natural means"—that is, by man—there is no replacement. Suppose, however, we cause the extinction of a species by ploughing up its habitat and growing crops, then surely we and the crops are the new forms that have replaced the old.

Should we feel responsible? We attribute the success of the dinosaurs partly to their large size and highly developed armour, and that of the birds to their ability to fly. With us, it is our highly developed brains. Having realized that we are, in so many ways, animals, with animal needs and impulses, we must also consider a few of the special results of having a human brain: we are able to think, and to learn from experience, and also to communicate abstract ideas. Our social behaviour has become far more complex and sophisticated than that of other primates. Our aesthetic sense and self-awareness are very highly developed; we are able to look at the progress we have made and appreciate the good things about it. We can also feel guilty about the progress we have not made and the harm we have done—

damage that all too often seems irreparable—to the earth and its inhabitants.

We have polluted the air, water, and earth with chemicals that we perceive to be harmful. But what does harmful mean? We could, if we liked, continue to say that DDT poisoning or the effects of atomic radiation on vegetation and animals (including man) are natural effects, brought about by the role we play in the natural environment. The dictionary says that something is *harmful* if it destroys or damages, so that by this definition radiation and germ warfare, air and water pollution, do harm. We are unable to reverse their harmful effects because reversing is like going backward in time, and we cannot do that. Any repairs we do are essentially re-adjustments and not reversals.

Why should we bother? The so-called conservationist attitude maintains that this damage is our responsibility. But if we go along with the weight of evidence and accept that we are only playing our natural role, why should we feel responsible for germ warfare, pollution, or even the extinction of other animals? During the course of geological time, literally millions of plants and animals have evolved and have died out and been replaced by new forms. We consider the mechanism of evolution to be a natural and non-directed process; we cannot and do not *blame* the dinosaurs for causing extinction of other animals. And yet conventional opinion still maintains that we are to blame for the extinction of animals that have died out during the period of our own life on earth. Is this logical?

Time In so many discussions about the "nature of man" or "man's impact on nature," time is the factor that so many people tend not to take into account. Let us use the familiar example. The dinosaurs lived on earth for more than 100 million years. Yet only a few million years ago there were no true men on earth; oceans covered the land where some of the world's major cities now stand; in some places where now there are oceans, there were perhaps deserts or mountain ranges.

The earth is constantly changing: continents drift apart, mountains are raised up, and eroded away unimaginably slowly. Sometimes natural changes are sudden and unpredictable: volcanoes thrust up lava from deep inside the earth with tremendous and terrifying violence.

On average, however, the time that we have been on earth has been a period of concentrated change. Some of the changes that have occurred are directly due to us; others are nothing to do with us at all. What is more, the speed at which changes take place appears to be accelerating. This acceleration is in fact partly an illusion, caused by the tremendous speeding up of communications since the invention of radio and long-distance telegraph. Distances and time appear to be telescoped. In this kind of world, it is not surprising that we cannot conceive of the enormity of geological time, because if we could, we might get things a little more into proportion. After all, in another 10 million years the sea will have washed most of man's creations away: bricks and concrete will have been redeposited under the sea as

The fish (*top left*) died because of changes in their environment caused by industrial effluents. The trilobites (*above*) also died of changes in the environment, but by causes unknown. Changes in temperature, and influx of noxious materials are common proven causes of wholesale deaths in fossil populations. These phenomena also cause what we call pollution *today*.

Radiation, in the form of cosmic rays from the sun may be responsible for some of the changes in genetic structure that have led to evolution. The trees (*below left*) have been destroyed within a radius of forty metres from a radiation source; the oak leaves (*below*) have been exposed to varying amounts of gamma rays. Is this damage or is it a visible example of evolution?

sandstone. We shall be extinct and some other species will probably be faced with the problems of conserving nature.

The Usual Stumbling Block An increasingly large number of scientists are advocating conservation and stressing the urgency of putting a really large-scale plan into practice. There is no doubt in the minds of the scientists that the only efficient conservation programme is one rigidly based on the laws of ecology. The public would, no doubt, accept this in theory. But of course we know that accepting a new idea in theory is quite different from changing our well-worn patterns of thought to come to terms with it in practice. Conservation, which seems so innocuous, has come up against the same old stumbling blocks. We are quite happy to work within ecological laws when we are planning to conserve other wild life; the trouble arises when we try to solve the pressing problems of *human* conservation. We have, it appears, learnt nothing from Galileo or Darwin. Despite all evidence to the contrary, we are still convinced that we are unique and therefore exempt from ecological laws. If we were really prepared to accept the new ideas, we should be prepared to apply the rules to ourselves as well; we should rarely try to save or prolong lives. Antibiotics and organ transplants would not be thought of; after all, endemic diseases are both efficient mechanisms of natural selection and controllers of population, as is food shortage. We should therefore accept—even welcome—epidemics and periodical large-scale famines; they would help enormously to keep the population down.

We might even practise on ourselves some of the modern methods we apply to livestock—for example, cropping (the selective killing of a proportion of animals either for use as food or because their numbers are outstripping their own food supply—see Chapter 6).

We should return to using methods of selective breeding. It is not so long since they were practised in America on Negro slaves, who were bred for physical strength, the so-called "Buck" Negro being used for breeding because of his size and virility. Even more recently there was another attempt at selective breeding, this time in order to produce a master race—the Herren-volk of Hitler's Germany. Aldous Huxley satirized selective breeding of humans in his novel *Brave New World* (1932). We ought to ask ourselves why these ideas are abhorrent to us and why ecological laws, when applied to the human race, become repulsive. We breed animals in hatcheries. Why not human beings?

It appears that even if we are going to practise conservation we are not going to abide by all the rules. It may therefore be a good idea at least to clarify our motives. A good deal is talked about "preserving the balance of nature" and "the love of wild life" that we can no longer accept so glibly; *we are not all that altruistic*. If we are honest, we must admit that our main thoughts are for ourselves—our own species' survival, our own pleasure and comfort, and even, at times, simply our own clear conscience. (Space for recreation, fresh air, and natural beauty are all necessary for our comfort and provide some of our greatest pleasures.) Without conservation what have we to look forward to in the long term?

At the moment, while there is still enough potential space and food, we can spare a thought for aesthetics, the preservation of other species, and so forth. But we are a fast-multiplying and terribly aggressive species. What is more, we are almost the only animal that kills its own kind wholesale for territory and prestige. Of course, with typical human cunning we call our weapons of aggression "deterrent" and our greed for mastery over territory "defence," but the old animal instincts still remain. As the pressure on resources and space becomes greater, competition for what is left will become fiercer. If a major plan of conservation has to wait until the public gradually comes to terms with the idea, hunger and overcrowding may well have already driven us to war on an unimaginable scale. Perhaps an ultimate holocaust is the logical and natural outcome of our role in the natural environment, but conservation is a much more attractive alternative.

To say that a crime such as the razing of Hiroshima could not happen today is self-delusion; it ignores human aggression and greed, and forgets that the nuclear arms race is as much with us as ever. We have no right to be complacent.

We will now look at Conservation through the eyes of the wildlife preservationists, whose aim is to alert people to the plight of rare animals and plants, and to try to prevent unnecessary extinctions where possible. Above: The original wild man of Borneo, an orang-utan whose name means "man of the woods" in Malay. It is the rarest of the great apes, threatened with extinction because of its popularity and charm. Despite stringent controls, many orang-utans are smuggled out and sold abroad every year.

CHAPTER 4

WILDLIFE GIVES WAY

As our own civilization spreads across the earth, wild life is often the innocent victim. Large numbers of animals have become extinct since records first began and the extinction process is known to be speeding up.

Many books on conservation begin with statements such as, "During the past 2000 years, at least 100 different forms of mammals have become extinct in various parts of the world," or, "Over the last 300 years we have exterminated more than 200 forms of birds and mammals." Claims such as these are, as we shall see, rather meaningless in themselves and are usually intended to shock the reader. In the last chapter we agreed that man is largely to blame for the plight of other species, and that we have an obligation to prevent this plight from getting worse, if we can. But unless we understand how and why animals are threatened, we cannot hope to preserve wild life. Let us look for a moment at the sensationalists' cries of despair. What do they mean when they say that more than 200 bird and mammal forms have become extinct? What is a form? Does it mean species or genus? Do they themselves know what it means? It is in fact meaningless, because it is impossible to be definite about what happened before living things were properly classified.

The method of classifying living things is based on that of the Swedish botanist Carl von Linné (1707–1778), also known as Linnaeus. He gave every plant he studied two names, the first being the name of the genus (or generic name) and the second the name of the species (or specific name). By using these two names, it is theoretically possible to pin down any animal or plant and give it an accurate identity. Take the example *Canis familiaris*, the domestic dog. The first name, *Canis* (with a capital C), is the generic name for dogs; *familiaris* (with a small f) is the particular kind of species of dog—the common dog. Sometimes the specific name refers to the area where the animal is found—for instance, *Dama mesopotamica*, the Mesopotamian fallow deer; sometimes a species is named after its discoverer or after an eminent scientist—for example, *Tapirus bairdii* (Baird's tapir); then again a characteristic feature may be pinpointed and translated into Latin or Greek—such as *Ursus horribilis*, the American Grizzly Bear.

Living things are then grouped into larger units called *families*, and families are grouped together into *orders*; finally several orders are grouped into one major division called a *phylum*. It must be stressed that we classify in order to simplify the job of fitting the world's living things into a pattern. The species is taken as the basis of classification, but even this is difficult to define, because all species are evolving and continually changing. The nearest we can get to a definition is to say that if two animals or plants breed in the wild and produce live and fertile offspring, then they are of the same species. By this rule the horse (*Equus caballus*) and the donkey (*Equus asinus*) are said to belong to two different species because, although they can interbreed, their offspring—the mule—is itself sterile. As time passes, a single species may become extinct or may evolve into several new species. There will be a stage during this evolution when there will be several forms very closely related to each other. A good example of this is the tiger, whose scientific name is *Panthera tigris*. There are many varieties of tiger that are still similar enough to belong to the same species but now have different geographical ranges and are slowly developing other differences too: thus the Sumatran tiger is called *Panthera tigris sumatrae*, while the Bali tiger is called *Panthera tigris balica*, and so on. This third name is that of the sub-species; animals from two different sub-species could theoretically breed, but no longer do so in the wild because they have become separated from each other in various ways. Most living things are given only two names, however, and this is sufficient to identify them.

Extinction　When a species consistently fails to produce enough young in each generation to keep pace with the death rate, it eventually becomes extinct. The rate of extinction can be fast or slow, depending on the causes. There are, as we know, no hard and fast rules about either extinction rates or the probable life span of a species. But the following tentative calculation has been made: in 1680 a bird species could expect an existence of 40,000 years, but in 1964 its life expectancy would be only about 16,000 years.

This is yet another generalized statement. It is designed to make the reader aware that the probable life expectancy of a species (not of an individual) is greatly reduced today as compared with 300 years ago. The implication is that we are responsible. As we cannot argue against this, the best thing we can do is to set out the facts as far as they are known.

There are two kinds of extinction. One is caused by direct assault, the other is caused indirectly by interference with an animal's habitat. First, we shall deal with extinction by direct assault.

For thousands of years we have killed animals for food and clothing, and indeed for sport—as we mentioned in the first chapter. But in fact we can trace an ascending curve of slaughter that is directly related to technical improvements in weapons, and also in the means of travel. Even before the Industrial Revolution, improvements in sailing ships enabled men to make extended voyages to all parts of the world, thus opening up new opportunities

The bas-relief from Nineveh, Iraq, (above) shows that lions were hunted for sport in the time of Ashurbanipal, King of Assyria. This probably contributed to their disappearance from the Near East where they were once common. Below: Polar bears are menaced by modern hunting methods using helicopters for spotting them on ice-floes.

for killing, although still with crude weapons. But with the Industrial Revolution the curve of slaughter became even steeper, as mass-produced fire-arms and ammunition became available. Also, in the 19th century, one of the by-products of the Industrial Revolution was a sharp increase in the population of Europe, which in turn led to massive colonization of new areas, especially in North America. The invention of the locomotive and the steamship speeded up the slaughter in more ways than one, and today helicopters are used for spotting whales.

This is the technical background against which the carnage of recent years must be viewed; it provided means and opportunity, but what of the motive? In the following account of extinctions and near-extinctions, we make no attempt to be comprehensive, but only to show some of the ways in which these disasters have come about; for ease of remembering, however, we make use of a simple mnemonic—all the motives for killing begin with the letter F. They are Food, Fats, Finery (Fur and Feathers), Fun, Financial gain, and Fear. Sometimes these categories will overlap, but in general they are a good guide.

Killing for Food The target has normally been animals that congregated in such large numbers as to make commercial exploitation worthwhile; often their numbers were so great that no one believed that wholesale killing could reduce those numbers appreciably. Take the case of the passenger-pigeons, once the most numerous of all birds. When they migrated across North America the sky was darkened for over four hours by a flock more than a mile wide. One estimate in the 1850s put the size of a flock at well over 2000 million birds. How was it possible to reduce such a population to extinction? The answer was "greed." Passenger-pigeons were tasty and easy to shoot because they congregated in huge flocks. When they nested they took over entire forests; sometimes there were 100 nests in a single tree. Shoots were organized, and marketing became big business by about 1858. There were night "drives" to harvest the birds at their nesting places. Not only shotguns were used but also artillery—cannons and the forerunners of the machine-gun. One New York trader dealt in a daily turnover of 18,000 birds. In 1879 at least 1000 million birds were captured in Michigan alone. Even the passenger-pigeon could not stand up to this rate of depletion. Already by 1860 the breeding colonies—which had hitherto been enormous—had completely disappeared. The last nest observed in the wild was in 1894. The species became extinct when the last captive individual, a hen called Martha, died in 1914 in the Cincinnati Zoo.

The American bison—incorrectly but commonly called the *buffalo*—was once so numerous that the sight of its herds migrating south for winter was an awe-inspiring experience. One traveller in 1832 wrote of them, "As far as my eye could reach, the country seemed absolutely blackened by innumerable herds." Far into the 19th century, numbers were estimated at well over 60 million. The American Indians had succeeded in living off the buffalo without ever substantially reducing their numbers; they hunted them on horseback with bows and arrows or sometimes by driving the buffalo over cliffs during the migration. From these animals the Indians obtained many of their necessities. They used the skin to make their tepees, clothes, and moccasins. From the gut they made bow strings, and from the horn they made spoons; buffalo meat was their staple diet.

When the white settlers came west at the end of the 18th century, the situation slowly began to change. The Indians were offered steel knives, fire-arms, and whisky in exchange for buffalo skins, and they found they could kill the animals far more efficiently with fire-arms than with the bow and arrow. Then, during the building of the Union Pacific Railway in the 1860s the buffalo became the staple diet for the construction gangs. As we have already said in Chapter 1, buffalo shooting for the Union Pacific became a very profitable industry—for a while. That notable professional hunter William F. Cody, otherwise known as Buffalo Bill, accounted for 4280 buffalo over a period of 18 months—probably a world record. In just over 15 years the buffalo was all but exterminated; in the period 1870–5, at least two and a half million animals were killed every year. Although this slaughter continued without respite until buffalo shooting stopped being profitable, there is a grim climax to this tale. By 1883 only one herd of about

Mounted Sioux hunters, chasing buffalo. They used only spears and bows, swooping down the hillside and confusing their quarry before closing in for the kill.

10,000 buffalo remained, in North Dakota. One morning in September a party of hunters set out with the express purpose of exterminating what was left of this species; they shot 1000 beasts on the first day alone. By November the buffalo had just about ceased to exist in the wild.

The extermination of the buffalo had a secondary, ecological, effect. We have said that the Red Indian was very dependent on the buffalo for both food and other materials. The removal of the buffalo resulted in such hunger and hardship among the plains Indians that they ceased to be an obstacle to a complete take-over of their land by white men; the few Indians who survived were easily controlled and put into reserves. It is believed that the near-extermination of the buffalo was part of a deliberate government policy intended to secure two clearances for the price of one.

Giant tortoises are very primitive reptiles and they are found today on the Seychelles, Mauritius, and Aldabra islands in the Indian Ocean and the Galapagos Islands in the Pacific. They were much more widely distributed in the past, but they have long since disappeared from other parts of the tropics and subtropics. On these remote islands the tortoises survived because they had no predators before man came. So numerous were they on the Galapagos Islands during the 16th century, that the discoverer of the islands, the Spanish priest and explorer Fray Thomas de Berlanga, named them after the tortoises (*Galapago* is the Spanish for tortoise). These islands were also called by the name "Encantadas"—the enchanted islands.

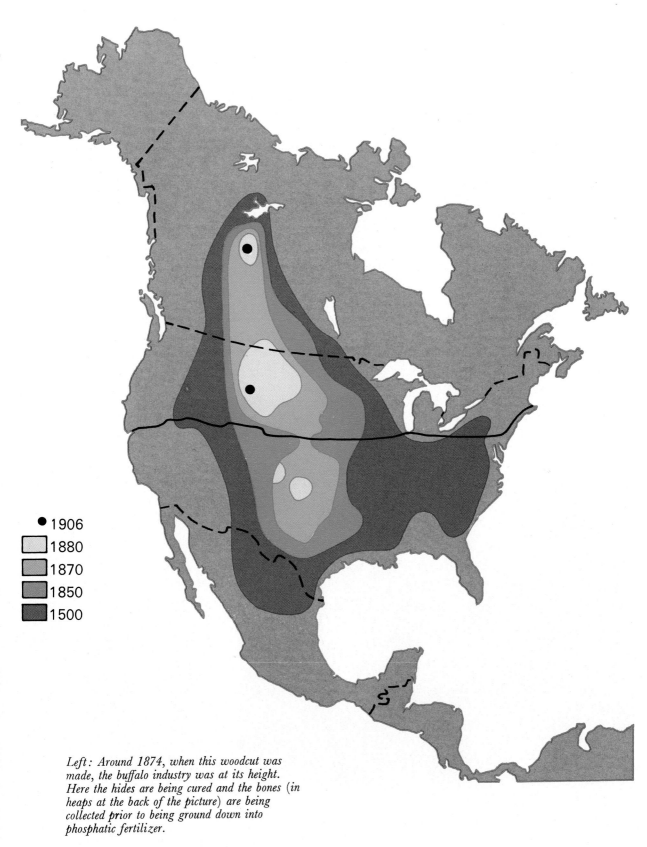

● 1906
1880
1870
1850
1500

*Left: Around 1874, when this woodcut was
made, the buffalo industry was at its height.
Here the hides are being cured and the bones (in
heaps at the back of the picture) are being
collected prior to being ground down into
phosphatic fertilizer.*

*Above: this map shows the progressive decrease
in the range of the American bison or buffalo,
due to heavy predation by white settlers.*

The sailors were most pleased with their discovery—the tortoises were delicious to eat, and the English buccaneer and navigator William Dampier said of them in 1697, "The land turtles were so numerous that five or six hundred men might subsist on them alone for several months without any other sort of provision." The tortoises' great misfortune was that, if kept damp and cool, they could survive without food or water down in the holds of ships for up to 21 months. Sailors used to collect 600–900 of the smallest and most succulent and take them aboard. The American Captain Porter, describing victualling operations at Galapagos during the early 1800s, said: "In four days we had as many on board as would weigh about fourteen tons. They were piled up on the quarter deck for a few days with an awning spread over to shield them from the sun, which renders them very restless, in order that they might have time to discharge the contents of their stomachs; afterwards they were stowed away below as you would stow any other provisions." The cook would simply kill them as required.

Charles Darwin found the Galapagos tortoise still quite numerous when he visited the islands in *HMS Beagle* in 1835. He noted that they got their fresh water by eating spring cactus leaves, because the only fresh water on most of the islands was in the form of temporary pools. He was struck by the sight of "the huge reptiles, surrounded by black lava, leafless shrubs and large cacti, that seemed to my fancy like some antediluvian animals."

At about the same time as the Galapagos Islands were discovered, explorers landed on the Seychelles. There they found giant tortoises living in similarly large numbers. The French explorer Lequat, writing in 1691, said

Tortoises and turtles are very primitive reptiles and of great interest to biologists. They are vulnerable as long as man continues to cultivate a taste for them. The Galapagos giant tortoise (left) was killed only for its liver; the rest of the beast was left to rot. Right: The green turtle; its eggs are such a delicacy that they are protected by being transferred from the nests to special hatcheries.

of the Island of Rodriguez in the Mauritius group: "There are such plenty of land turtles in this isle that sometimes you see two or three thousand of them in a flock, so that you may go above 100 paces on their back." One hundred and fifty years later the giant tortoise had been completely wiped out from Rodriguez and other islands of the group. Since man has settled on almost all other islands where the giant tortoises live, they have become even rarer. They are still prized for their meat and of course for their eggs, and sometimes an animal is killed by piercing its shell simply in order to extract the liver, which is a special delicacy. The younger animals are pestered and killed by introduced dogs and rats, and they are in great need of protection. They have always been infrequent breeders, because they did not need to produce many young in an environment free from predators. But in this new situation, where there are predators on all sides, it is doubtful whether they can survive. Seychelles islanders keep a few as pets, and zoos are attempting to breed them in captivity. We shall be talking about this in the next chapter.

The eggs of many reptiles and birds are good sources of protein, and are much sought after. Not only tortoises suffer: turtles, too, are hunted, both for their flesh and for their eggs, and turtle soup is a delicacy that is becoming more and more scarce.

Many birds are easy victims of the nest robber, because the birds themselves are almost always easy to shoot or to scare away from the eggs they are incubating. Take the case of the Laysan albatross, which breeds on the Hawaiian island of the same name. This is one of the many kinds of sea birds

that breed on remote Pacific islands. Each female lays only one egg a year, which the islanders collect, carting millions of eggs away in trucks and barrows. This animal harvest brings the Laysan islanders a living; but, with no long-term planning for allowing at least a proportion of the eggs to hatch, how long will it continue to be profitable?

Because of their fearlessness, island-dwelling animals are often much easier to trap than mainland ones. The dodo (Portuguese *doudo*, meaning stupid) was a victim of its own fearlessness; sailors wrote incredulously of the way in which the dodos on Mauritius just sat and allowed themselves to be captured and killed. The birds (and indeed the reptiles and other animals too) of the Galapagos and Aldabra islands are equally fearless, so that these islands are favourite places for organized egg-hunting. Another island where organized bird-nesting is carried out is Nightingale Island, of the Tristan da Cunha group in the South Atlantic. Every September the Tristan islanders cross 25 miles to Nightingale Island to collect rock-hopper penguin eggs and guano. They return each April to collect the birds, which are a source of oil. They have to make this dangerous journey because their own native rock-hopper, once so numerous on Tristan, is now reduced to two rookeries.

Killing for Fats   The hunting of marine animals for fats has a long history, mostly of gross over-exploitation, and there are many stories to be told about excessive sealing and whaling in both northern and southern seas. These can be summarized by considering the fate of the southern blue whale. Apart from being the largest animal that has ever existed, the blue whale is commercially the most profitable animal in existence: a female 89 feet long and weighing 120 tons has yielded over 27 tons of oil, half from the blubber and half from the meat and bones. The composition of whale-oil is exactly the same as that of groundnuts or peanuts, but it has so far been cheaper and quicker to kill large whales than to cultivate large areas of a tropical crop that would produce the same yield. In Chapter 8 we shall be talking more about the importance of oilseed crops.

We have mentioned the impact of technology on killing, and here is a supreme example. Up to the beginning of this century the blue whale was immune from capture. Weapons and ships were unequal to the task until the steam whale-catcher had been developed to the point where it could tirelessly pursue whales in rough seas. The explosive harpoon had been developed in 1865 for use in northern waters. Then, in 1905, the harpoon gun was mounted on powerful whale-catchers, and put to work in the waters surrounding South Georgia. Another interesting technological feature was the inclusion in the catcher's machinery of a steam-driven air compressor. The reason for this compressor is that a blue whale, as well as other and smaller members of the same genus, sinks when it is dead; the only way, therefore, to keep a dead blue whale afloat, so that it can be towed in for processing, is to thrust a hollow lance into its belly and blow it up with compressed air. (The hole made by the lance is plugged with cotton waste soaked in kerosene; if any other oil is used, wandering albatross will pull the plug out and the whale will sink.)

The stock of southern blue whales at the beginning of this century has been estimated to be about 150,000. By 1961, after years of intensive whaling (first from land stations, and later from floating factory ships with their attendant catchers), the stock was reduced to an estimated minimum of 930 and a maximum of 2800. It is well known that if a population of animals falls below a certain level, it fails to recover. No one knows what the critical level is for blue whales. They may be doomed or they may recover; but because the few remaining whales are spread out over millions of square miles of ocean, there is a real possibility that males and females will fail to find each other during the breeding season. If this should happen, then there is no hope for this magnificent species. Meanwhile the practice of killing the goose that lays the golden eggs has shifted to an intensified slaughter of smaller whales of the same genus, such as fin, sei, and humpback whales, and there is already evidence that these whales too are rapidly declining.

Killing for Finery: Fur   Some seals, too, are hunted for their fat, but more are, or have been, hunted for their fur. The most highly prized fur seal, the Pribilof or Alaska fur seal, is a native of the Bering Sea. It was far more numerous at the turn of the century than it is now; almost 4 million were slaughtered between 1908 and 1910 by the Japanese, and the stock was endangered. Because of its commercial importance, the U.S. government assumed control in 1911, and after a resting period to enable the stock to recover, the killing is now regulated at 65,000 seals a year, so that it is no longer in danger of extinction.

The Guadalupe fur seal, however, is still in great danger, though it is no longer exploited commercially. The chief period of exploitation of this seal was in the 18th and 19th centuries, when enormous numbers of them lived off the Pacific coast of America. In 1805, about 80,000 animals were slaughtered for fur off the California coast. This kind of ravaging continued without control until, by the end of the 19th century, harvesting was no longer profitable. By then, the Guadalupe fur seal was very rare. After 1880 it was sighted only occasionally until in 1954 a breeding colony was discovered in a cave on its native Guadalupe Island; and the population now appears to be in the region of 200–500. But this seal is by no means out of danger; in fact it is doubtful whether the species can survive. Its close relative, the Juan Fernandez fur seal, is even closer to extinction. In 1792 it was estimated that there were about 3 million of them on Juan Fernandez Island, off the coast of Chile, but extensive hunting almost exterminated them and the latest estimate is put at about 50 individuals.

Harp or Greenland seals are found in the open arctic seas; they migrate north in the summer and come south in the spring for the breeding season. They are hunted in enormous numbers for meat and oil as well as for their fur and leather. But it is the coat of the baby seals that is most prized—either

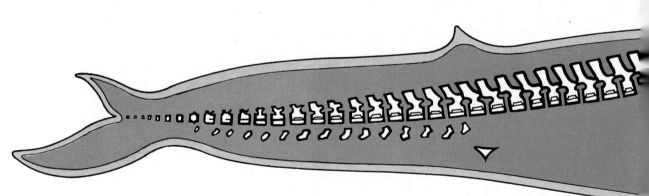

Above: The Laysan albatross, one of the victims of the Hawaiian Islands egg industry. Above centre: A similar industry flourishes—for the moment—on several Seychelles Islands; eggs collected from the nests of the sooty tern, boxed ready for marketing. Like the Laysan and even rarer Steller's albatross, sooty terns lay only one egg per year.

Far right: Man's technical skill has triumphed over the blue whale, largest of all mammals. The dead whale has been towed alongside the boat and air is being pumped into it to keep it afloat Below: Diagram of a blue whale shows blubber (grey), skeleton, and muscle (red); all exploited commercially. A man (corner) gives an idea of size.

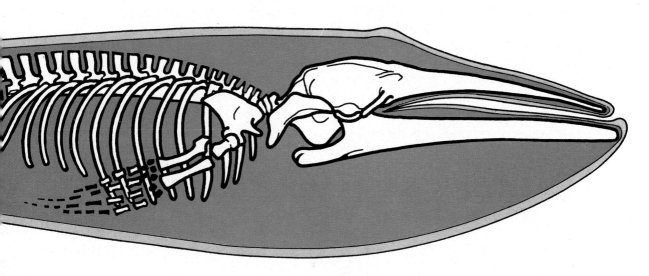

the first "whitecoat" of the new-born pup, or the grey and softer "beater" that replaces the whitecoat. The largest kill on record was in 1831, when 687,000 seals were killed. The present annual kill is about 80,000 adults and about 180,000 pups. The young are known to the sealers as "bedlamers"; this has nothing to do with Bedlam, the infamous lunatic asylum, but comes from the French "Bête de la mer," the name given to harp seals by 15th- and 16th-century Breton settlers in Canada.

One of the principal objections to sealing is the way in which it is often done. The public imagination has recently been caught by what it feels to be the brutal way in which many types of seal are hunted. They are clubbed on the head, and often merely stunned, and then they are skinned alive. More often, however, they are shot; detailed instructions are given in the pamphlet *Sealing in U.K. and Canadian Waters* (1968), of the exact calibre of rifle to use and of the precise position on the head to aim at. A very close range is recommended—one inch, if the animal is approachable. Seals are very awkward on land and it is quite easy to cut off their access to the sea and then to shoot them.

No animal, whether a land- or water-living species, can expect to be left alone if it sports a fur coat of any beauty. Many of the great cats are endangered for this reason; they are the quarry of both fur hunters and trophy seekers. One of the most attractive members of the leopard family is the snow leopard. It is an Asian variety and tends to be more arboreal than its African cousins. It is now very rare—so rare, in fact, that an American fashion house had this to say of it in an advertisement. They listed 88 different types of animal from which fur coats are made and continued, "Max Bogen regret that no. 17 is no longer available. Unfortunately, a Himalayan snow leopard perfect enough to become a Max Bogen fur coat has not been sighted in over 2 years. But you may be sure that when the right one comes along, it'll end up at Max Bogen."

The World Wildlife Fund's former executive director Herbert H. Mills emphasized the problem when he said: "Women of the world hold the future of such wild creatures in their hands. . . . Status symbols being what they are, and with the buying power of today, fashion trends can spell complete destruction to any wild thing that becomes the whim of fad and fashion."

The great cats breed fairly frequently; one pair may produce up to 20 young in a lifetime. Many of them have no natural enemy except disease, so that—in theory at least—there is no real reason why the excess should not be exploited by man for fur coats, rugs, or even bath-mats. But the trouble is that field conservationists cannot control hunting to within such fine limits. It is probably wiser therefore to put complete rather than partial protection on the killing of cats for fur. Even so, complete protection has very little effect on any animal when poachers are determined and cunning enough. Such are the poachers that roam the Florida Everglades in an increasingly difficult search for alligators. There are an estimated 1000 poachers still at work in spite of a law forbidding the killing of the American alligator.

Unfortunately, alligator skins are higly prized in the leather and souvenir trade. One report says that over 50,000 were poached in the USA in 1966. Unless this particular status symbol is superseded by another less destructive one the alligator is unlikely to survive. An ex-poacher is on record as saying, not long ago, "I wouldn't give the 'gator more than 3 or 4 years. . . . They'll kill until they get the last of them."

Killing for Finery: Feathers   Another animal whose skin can be turned into rather smart handbags is the African ostrich. At one time, however, the ostrich was not sought after for its leather, but for its tail feathers, which became a tremendous fashion fad that lasted over the turn of the century right up to World War I. In 1912, about 160 tons of feathers were sold in France alone. They were made into hat trimmings, floating feather boas, and fans for fan dancers and great ladies. Ostriches in the wild are vicious beasts, and can give a very nasty kick with their long legs. So it was naturally easier to shoot the birds than to risk severe injury by capturing them and plucking out their tail feathers. But a few enterprising businessmen realized at about this time that farming the ostrich would be profitable—after all, tail feathers can be plucked and they will grow again. Ostrich farms grew up in a few places; there is still a famous one at Uitshoorn in the Cape Province of South Africa. Unfortunately for the farmers, the fashion suddenly changed, as is its whim, and the bottom dropped out of the market in ostrich feathers; they were too expensive for most people during World War I. But the ostrich, which had been brought to the brink of extinction, was saved.

Another bird persecuted for its tail feathers is the bird of paradise, a native of the Molucca Islands. Legend had it that this bird never alighted, but spent its whole life on the wing, feeding on air and the rays of the sun. For this reason, it was named *Paradisa apoda* (the specific name means "without feet"). The bird of paradise has feet like any other bird, but it also has very beautiful tail plumage that, if plucked, will grow again in about a year. Naturally, as with the ostrich, it is much easier to shoot it. This is done with special blunt-tipped arrows so as not to damage the plumage.

While only the Moluccans coveted the feathers for head-dresses, this bird was not in danger, and although there was a trade in feathers up to World War I, the bird of paradise was rigidly protected. But since 1957 the Moluccas have become strategic keypoints for the movements of Indonesian troops, and the bird of paradise has suddenly and unwittingly become a status symbol. When an official tour is made of the Moluccas by any high-ranking army official, the first thing he will do is ask for a "Bouroung Tjendrawasih" —a bird of paradise. The subordinates, anxious for promotion, will naturally do all they can to obtain one, even though they are well aware that the bird is protected by law. Recent figures show that a single skin will fetch up to 670 U.S. dollars; a stuffed bird mounted on a perch can be sold for as much as 2200 dollars at the port of Djakarta.

If the bird of paradise does manage to survive this slaughter it will be for a

Above: A prospective buyer in a warehouse in Nairobi, selecting from the beautifully mounted skins of zebra, leopard and antelope. The trophy industry is a good source of revenue for Kenya. Below: The whitecoat pup of the harp or greenland seal, the main target of commercial exploiters.

Above: The Snow Leopard which lives in the high mountains of China, India and the USSR is one of the most beautiful of the great cats. This does not go unnoticed by fur traders; pelts fetched $175 in 1967. There are probably no more than 500 left in the Himalayan part of their range. Left: The Alligator gets its name from El lagarto "the lizard" in Spanish. But alligators and crocodiles are not lizards, but archosaurs—related to dinosaurs and to the remote ancestors of birds. They are the last of the "ruling reptiles."

Above: Fans fashionable at the time of Queen Victoria's Golden Jubilee. They were trimmed with birds and butterflies, tortoise-shell, ostrich feathers and elephant ivory. Later in 1930, the ostrich feather fashion reached the most dizzy heights. Right: A huge head-dress being "supported" by long-suffering Jessie Matthews.

Right: The "gooseflesh" on this ostrich skin shows where the feathers have been plucked out. Ostrich feathers are not flight feathers as the ostrich has lost the power of flight. They are more like "nestling down" which flighted birds lose when they develop their flight plumage.

rather comic reason. The local hunters appear to know nothing about the sexual dimorphism in this species. (This means that the male and female look quite different.) In fact it is doubtful whether they even know that the modest brown female exists. They sell the mounted male birds as females if they have bent necks, and as males if they have straight necks. There is also another hope for the survival of the species; the full adult male plumage develops only at the end of the second year. This allows the male birds to breed before they are coveted and shot.

We cannot hope to talk about all the wild life on the danger list today. We cannot even list all the reasons why certain animals are persecuted until they cease to exist. Some of these reasons lie deep in tribal lore and legend. We cannot know why a particular beast or some part of it should be said to be endowed with magical, aphrodisiac, or healing powers. In some cases there is a definite factual basis for these powers: for instance, the head fat of the dugong or sea-cow does seem to cure the Malagasy people of headaches, and the efficacy of certain kinds of snake venom as a blood-clotting

agent is beyond doubt—but whether there is always sound medical evidence for healing powers is an open question. While people continue to believe in them, their unfortunate sources of supply will continue to be in danger. Of all the beasts to be endowed with mysterious powers, the rhinoceros is of course one of the unluckiest. Later in this book we shall be talking more about rhinos and attempts to save them from extinction. Suffice it to say, for the moment, that an animal whose horns are worth up to 2500 dollars in many parts of the East is in dire need of care and protection.

Killing for Fun In some affluent societies, hunting and fishing have become status symbols, particularly in countries where wild life is restricted to small areas; but it should be said in defence of the status seekers that, apart from undersized fish that are thrown back, most of the animals they kill make a useful protein supplement to their diet. But the souvenir industry has become a major racket. Alligators are stuffed and sold as souvenirs; elephants are killed for their tusks, and their feet are hollowed out and

These hunters (left) kill the elephant for food, but manage to make a reasonable sideline out of selling off its inedible parts to the souvenir industry. In workshops such as the one on the right, elephants' feet are polished and turned into useful objects. This year's fashion seems to be coffee tables and stools, with zebra-foot ashtrays running a close second.

turned into novelty elephant-foot umbrella stands or waste-paper baskets.

In the heyday of colonialism, administrators were responsible for the near-extinction of rhinos, the tiger, and several other great cats, and a host of other beasts, so that the newly independent countries are left with a somewhat depleted heritage. It is to be hoped that they will all realize the importance of their native faunas and try to control further irresponsible killing.

Killing for Financial Gain The live animal trade accounts for very large numbers of animals every year. Poachers are alert to the markets, and the rarer the animal species, the greater its market price to collectors. Perhaps the most lamentable case of wild animal smuggling is that of the orang-utan. Although there is now a complete ban on the export of orang-utans, and although they are very carefully guarded in the wild, the smuggling still goes on.

The orang-utan is not the only primate to be threatened by the wild animal trade. Various species of monkeys are required for medical research, and several types are being depleted by this new trade. In 1963 the veterinary department of London Airport recorded 42,000 monkeys passing through their hands.

Killing through Fear Many carnivores attack man as well as other animals and are—if there are weapons to hand—shot on sight. Crocodiles, tigers, wolves, bears, and great cats have been reduced enormously in this way. Even herbivores such as rhinos, elephants, and African buffalo can become extremely fierce if approached, especially when they are nursing their young. No one ventures into wild game territory without a rifle, if he can help it, and a man may be forgiven for shooting a killer before it attacks him. This is why it is so difficult, especially in the wilder regions of the world, to put dangerous animals on the list of protected species. Not only is there a risk that a carnivore will attack a man; there is also a constant fear that livestock will be assaulted. A farmer's stock is his livelihood and this must be protected before the predator.

One of the world's rarest animals is the thylacine or Tasmanian wolf, also called the Tasmanian tiger. This animal—which is in fact neither a wolf nor a tiger, but a marsupial—is the largest of the Australian carnivores, and was once very common over the whole of the Australian mainland as well as Tasmania, but was probably decimated by the smaller dingo back in the Pleistocene. It was later recognized as a sheep killer and from the early part of the 19th century it was the victim of highly organized persecution by farmers. As far back as 1832, an Australian newspaper reported it as rarely seen. The government, quite unaware of the uniqueness of the thylacine, offered bounties of £1 for each adult animal brought in, and 10 shillings for each subadult. Between 1888 and 1914, the government paid out 12,268 bounties. There is thought to have been an epidemic in 1910, perhaps of distemper, and this reduced the thylacine population still further. When the

Above: To be hunted to near-extinction for meat and hide (and because its tail makes an excellent fly whisk) was the fate of the South African white-tailed gnu. The last thousand or so survivors now live on a few reserves and farms.

Australian government eventually gave it protection in 1938, it must have been nearly extinct. It has now quite disappeared from the Australian mainland, although occasional authentic reports of it still come in from mountainous localities in Tasmania. Even in Tasmania, not one has been trapped since 1922. During the 1950s there were hardly any sightings of the animal itself, but there has been evidence that it still exists, from its tracks and characteristic kills. (The victim's chest is ripped open and the heart and lungs eaten; the thylacine also has a preference for blood-sucking.) Recent efforts to trap it in the interests of science have been unsuccessful: traps baited with kangaroo meat and bacon failed; one attempt, in which a live wallaby was used, nearly succeeded, but the thylacine escaped, leaving only bits of its fur as proof that it had been there at all.

Conservationists in Tasmania are still looking for it, and are confident that, given time and money, the thylacine will once again be discovered. Co-operation by farmers is expected and the government has offered compensation for any sheep it may kill.

Fear of Competition   Since the Boers settled in South Africa, the native ungulates (hoofed mammals) have suffered the consequences. No fewer than five forms of antelope and zebra have become extinct or almost extinct.

Left: The coyote is hunted as a pest because it kills man's livestock. In this picture it is eating a calf it has killed. Below: One of the finer pictures of the thylacine. Its amazing similarity to a true dog is an example of parallel evolution.

Right top: Slash and burn of tropical rainforest in Peru. Below: The soil erosion that follows deforestation for agriculture. This shows conservation's dilemma: in this chapter we see deforestation as a tragedy for wildlife, but in Chapter 8 our concern is focused on the people who go hungry when soil that seemed fertile is reduced to a dustbowl. Can we have it both ways?

Unfortunately, three antelopes and two zebras—one of which was the quagga, of which we shall have more to say on page 102—were competing with the Boers' own herds for the pasturelands of Cape Province, and were systematically destroyed. Actually two of the three antelopes—the bontebok and the white-tailed gnu—do survive today in small numbers, but only in captivity.

Indirect Extermination A large proportion of the wild life today in danger of extinction is threatened almost by default. Animals are the victims of our own species' ever-increasing need to expand, and this expansion often takes place without anyone giving a thought to its by-products. Clearly a lot of this is unavoidable—the spread of human industry, urbanization, and agriculture is inevitable; but in its wake many of the world's rarest, often most beautiful and curious, species suffer and become extinct.

One of the major causes of danger to wild life is the felling of primeval forest. In former times, forest spread densely over many areas of the world— not only in the tropics, but in temperate zones too. This climax vegetation has remained stable for a very long time and has allowed a network of stable ecosystems to develop; each one has its own complex of plant and animal life. We know very little about the habits of many of the inhabitants of the more remote jungles, because they tend to be shy and sometimes nocturnal, and are therefore very difficult to catch for study in captivity.

At the present time the extension of agriculture threatens a very large number of species with loss of habitat; already many of the rarer forms have been squeezed into a tighter and tighter habitat by the gradual cutting back of their natural forests, and several more face total extermination as the last of their forest ecosystems are being destroyed.

This is certainly the bleak picture in Malagasy (formerly Madagascar), which has a unique biological history. On this island live some extremely interesting animals found nowhere else in the world. These are the lemurs, which are relatives of the monkeys but much more primitive. They are adapted to life in the dense tropical forest that, until recently, covered most of the island. At one time there were lemurs on the African mainland, but they could not compete with the true monkeys, which are more agile and intelligent. The lemurs of Malagasy have been free from predators for many millions of years, ever since the island broke away from the mainland.

The rarest lemur of all is the tiny aye-aye—so rare that there may well be no more than 50 individuals left. (Incidentally, the aye-aye suffers not only from the destruction of its habitat, but also from being hunted as a witch and herald of death by the local people.) When numbers fall as low as this, it is very doubtful whether a species can be revived at all. However, successful attempts have been made with several other species (Chapter 5) and perhaps the present efforts to save the aye-aye will also have good results.

There are many ways of clearing forest, although very few of them actually result in the creation of long-term productive arable land (p. 175). After a year or two the land is already unproductive and this has resulted in progressive forest felling known as the "slash and burn" method, still widely practised. In this age-old system, a piece of ground is cleared of vegetation, cultivated for a few years, and then abandoned as soon as it ceases to be fertile. Meanwhile, the animal population is forced further into what is left of the forest, where of course it is up against competition from the animals already there. Of the many species to be threatened by slash and burn cultivation, we can mention only a few.

In South and Central America much of the tropical forest is being cleared; in Brazil 85 per cent of forest has given way to agricultural land. Great cats cannot survive in a constricted space; the jaguar, for instance, needs 60,000 acres in which to roam on its nocturnal hunts. Other dense-forest dwellers, such as the tapirs of Malaysia and Mexico, are threatened, as are also the pygmy chimpanzee of the Congo, the Central American spider monkey, and countless birds. The list of species threatened by loss of habitat is very long indeed.

The draining of swamps and lakes also causes loss of habitat. Water-birds have some chance of survival if they can re-establish themselves elsewhere; but amphibians such as frogs, toads, and newts are far less mobile, and unlikely to find new ponds in which to breed. For example, much of Upper

The bonobo or pygmy chimpanzee lives on the south bank of the Congo River, in humid forest. As it was not discovered until 1929 it is uncertain whether it is rare because its forest habitat has been partially destroyed by man, or because it has always had a very limited range.

Above right: The Australian lungfish, in danger of extinction by pollution of its stream habitat. Now a sanctuary has been set up in Queensland to protect this "living fossil," one of three surviving species of a type of fish that has changed little in over 300 million years. Far right: The flightless notornis of New Zealand, thought to be extinct. An expedition rediscovered about a hundred pairs in a remote valley, where they are still endangered by predators and may not survive long.

Right: Whether the Lacandon Indians of Mexico are or are not the descendants of the Mayas, they are of great interest to geneticists studying the effects of inbreeding. Near right: A young man whose sense of taste is being tested. A high proportion of non-tasters and albinos (far right) are genetical indications of inbreeding.

Left: These deformed frogs were discovered in a ditch into which the Amsterdam Nuclear Research Station dumped its waste. Their ditch habitat has been destroyed by carelessness in the disposal of highly dangerous material, and from this we can learn two lessons. First, it is imperative that better methods be found to render this waste harmless—especially with increasing use of nuclear power. Second, no animal—man included—is immune to the dangers of radiation.

Galilee in Israel was a fetid malarial swamp 30 years ago. When it was drained to make way for agriculture, the most likely victims were amphibians and turtles; but fortunately these were spared by setting aside part of the region as a reserve.

In other parts of the world, water-dwelling species are threatened by man-made disturbance. For instance, in Guatemala the Lake Atitlán grebe is on the danger list mainly because its life is being made unbearable by speed-boats.

Pollution   Another major cause of indirect extermination is pollution. There are various types of pollutants, and farmers and conservationists are increasingly concerned about the effects of chemicals used in agriculture. One well-known pesticide is DDT, which has recently been found to be indestructible; a penguin caught as far away as Antarctica was found to contain DDT in its fat. We shall be talking about pesticides more in relation to our environment on page 178. Some of the by-products of industry should, however, be mentioned here. For instance, the industrial effluent from the town of Irkutsk is pouring into Lake Baikal in the USSR. This lake is the largest and deepest body of fresh water in the world; it contains one fifth of all freshwater reserves and in the lake lives the world's only freshwater seal as well as over 700 other species that are *endemic*—that is, they live nowhere else. Not only is pollution destroying some of this fauna, but it also threatens to cause climatic changes that could result in the advance of the Gobi Desert, as well as making dangerous inroads into our water supply.

Although no actual extinctions have as yet been caused by radio-activity, the dangers of radiation must be stressed, and further contamination of the earth by irresponsible people should be prevented.

Interference   When a non-native species is introduced into an area, there will often be disastrous results that were not predicted at all. As we have seen, many island faunas have been ravaged by dogs and rats, accidentally introduced from trading ships. In other cases, introduction of non-native species has been by design, sometimes with the express intention of controlling a pest. Unfortunately, many early experiments in biological control have ended badly. For example, there is a sad story of the mongoose, introduced into Jamaica in the 1870s. The idea was to set the mongoose onto the black rats, which were something of a plague on the island and a menace to the sugar-cane planters. Several other animals had been tried, including ferrets and large toads (which feed on baby rats), but they were unable to cope with the rat population. Unfortunately, the chosen mongooses were not wild specimens, but were born and bred in captivity in London. They had never seen a rat, and when they reached Jamaica they were more frightened of the rats than the rats were of them. Later in the same year some mongooses despatched direct from India were released in Jamaica and they soon got most of the rats under control. Some of the rats, however, quickly adapted to predation by the mongoose by taking to the trees and eating tree-living birds. After a time, too, the rat supply became insufficient, so that the mongooses began eating other things easier to come by, such as eggs, and they succeeded in exterminating several local reptiles and birds.

A well-adjusted habitat can even be unwittingly destroyed by domestic dogs and cats. Usually domesticated animals remain at home or within the settlement, but sometimes an animal leaves a settlement and becomes *feral* (from the Latin *fera*, a wild beast). When a sheepdog begins worrying sheep, this is a sign that the dog is reverting to the wild state; the only remedy is to shoot it without delay. If a dog or cat becomes feral, it naturally attacks wild life, often with serious consequences. Horses, too, can become feral and compete for grazing with the native fauna.

Many of the Australian marsupials have had their habitat destroyed by feral dogs and cats. Also, the dingo, a true dog that was introduced into Australia by the Aborigines, was originally domesticated but some of them went feral. Thus dingoes can be either domestic or wild, and the wild ones do a great deal of damage.

Natural Extinction   Sometimes a species dies out for no obvious reason; the usual causes of extinction—such as over-exploitation, disease, or failure to compete with other animals, or to adapt to a changing environment—do not seem to fit. But there is one other reason, and this is a condition known as *racial senescence*, in which the ability of a species to survive seems to have become played out. This senescence is connected with the organization of the enormous numbers of genes that determine heredity. Every species needs a constant reshuffling of its genes if it is to produce a big enough variety of offspring to ensure its adaptability to a changing environment. This supply of genes is commonly called the *gene pool*. If the pool is too small, the variations that enable a species to survive are much reduced, especially in a small natural population. Then the weak characteristics in its genetic make-up, such as a tendency to disease or to poor hearing, are no longer masked by the stronger features, and the inevitable result is that the species will die out.

A good example, among humans this time, is the Lacandon Indians of Central America, an isolated tribe numbering no more than 300. They have not intermarried with outsiders ever since the break-up of the Mayan Empire, 1000 years ago. Today the Lacandones are extremely inbred so that their gene pool is much reduced. They suffer from serious disabilities, their resistance to disease is very low, and unless they enlarge their gene pool by inter-marriage they are doomed to eventual extinction.

This is an example of racial senescence in humans, but the laws of genetics apply not only to humans, but to the rest of the animal and plant kingdoms. It is evident therefore that a knowledge of genetics is a necessary part of the equipment of a wild-life conservationist, and, as we shall see in the next chapter, this knowledge is being used in a variety of interesting and unexpected ways.

Above: This Chartley Bull belongs to a herd that has been kept and bred in captivity since the year 1248. They are probably the descendants of the original white cattle, introduced into Britain by the Romans, possibly as sacrificial animals.

CHAPTER 5

RESCUE BY CAPTIVITY

Clearly, much of the world's wild life is in need of immediate care and protection; the question is how to do it. This is one of the main concerns of a scientific body called the International Union for the Conservation of Nature and Natural Resources (known as the IUCN). Its headquarters are in Switzerland, and it operates a department, called the Survival Service Commission, that maintains contact with conservationists all over the world. The commission collects and collates information from field officers working on fauna preservation, from amateur naturalists, and indeed from anyone who has the time and ability to make detailed and accurate surveys of the state of any one or more species. Sometimes a survey such as this is easy to accomplish; for example, it is not difficult to make a count of an animal that lives in only small numbers on one island. But it is far more difficult to estimate accurately the numbers of a migratory animal or a form whose range is scattered over a wide area. If the species to be counted is rare in any case, and is shy and nocturnal as well, no clear idea of numbers can be gained at all; the best that can be done is to report on whether such an animal seems to be extinct or not.

Whatever information can be gathered is sent at intervals to the headquarters of the IUCN and the Survival Service Commission compiles a loose-leaf record called the *Red Data Book*, which is sent to subscribers. Fresh information sheets are sent out when there is anything new to report, and every effort is made to keep the book up to date. But if their information (and hence ours) is sometimes out of date, it is because surveys cannot always be made often enough, and the fortunes of many species may change considerably over a short period of time.

A typical page of the Red Data Book lists the name of a species or subspecies and follows this with information on its present and former distribution, its present status—if rare, very rare or perhaps merely a small local population that was never numerous. Then come details (if known) of its estimated numbers, its breeding rate in the wild and in captivity, the reasons for its decline, and whether killed deliberately or endangered indirectly. The rest of the page is devoted to conservation measures—those already undertaken (if any), those proposed (if any), and to numbers held and bred in captivity.

At present there are two Red Data Books, one on mammals and one on birds; further volumes on amphibians, reptiles, and plants are in preparation. Invertebrates are simply too numerous to be catalogued in this way, and no Red Book is planned for them, though there is an extremely long and varied list of rare invertebrates which are very interesting to zoologists as they have no close relatives—they are evolutionary mysteries.

There are three main ways in which wild life can be preserved. The first is by according legal protection to the species itself. The second is to surround the habitat of one or several species with a real or imaginary fence and thus to protect the habitat plus the wild life inside it. The third is to remove a breeding stock from the natural habitat and breed from this stock in captivity under controlled conditions: the captive-bred offspring may eventually be returned to the wild if its numbers have recovered sufficiently to give them a reasonable chance of its survival under natural conditions.

Captive Breeding   When a species is in danger of extermination, a fairly practical solution is to transfer a breeding stock to a zoo. This is not ecologically ideal, because all zoos, however good, provide an artificial environment; but it is preferable to losing a species altogether. Zoos exist primarily for

Left : London Zoo in 1866—tiny cages, crowds of visitors—far from ideal conditions for all concerned. Right : Longleat Lion Park, England. Spacious, but full of attempts to imitate African game reserves—for profit, not for conservation.

Right : These two giant pandas appear to have met too late. The once-hopeful zoo authorities have had to realize that Chi-Chi and An-An are now middle aged and not as spry as they used to be. This is one of the problems of captive breeding.

exhibiting animals to the public. Indeed in the 19th century the aim of a zoo was to exhibit one specimen of as many different species as possible; breeding was neglected almost completely. Nowadays, however zoos make a point of breeding animals in captivity, and this is often far from easy. One of the many problems that arise is space. Many zoos are in cities and they simply cannot afford the room necessary for building up large herds of animals. This is where privately owned zoos with a good deal of space, such as Woburn Abbey in England, are particularly useful.

Because many of the larger zoos rely on the public in order to keep going, they are bound to exhibit the more popular, large, and furry creatures that are the apple of the public's eye. In the background however, the zoo staff are perhaps more interested in the shy, nocturnal beasts and the rare species, and especially in inducing them to breed. It is difficult to keep some of these in captivity for any length of time even without attempting to breed them, and breeding successes are still rather patchy. (Basle zoo has one of the best records, with 47 of its 79 species breeding regularly.)

What are the problems of breeding in captivity? As we saw in the last chapter, a species that has been reduced to a very few individuals is limited by having a small gene pool. Zoos realize this and make every effort to introduce their members to strangers of the same species in other zoos.

And, of course, in the case of really rare animals there is no other way of increasing the stock, except by introducing single animals from one zoo or another. In the summer of 1968 for example, the female giant panda Chi Chi, an inmate of London Zoo, was flown to Moscow and introduced to An An, a male inmate of Moscow zoo—but without success. The return match took place from September 1968—again without issue.

Diet is extremely important if a species is to be healthy enough to breed successfully. It is not always essential to provide an animal with the actual ingredients of its natural diet, but it is important to make sure that animals get the correct balance of protein, carbohydrates, fats, minerals, vitamins, and trace elements. There are some animals, however, that do need specific food; the koala, for instance, feeds only on eucalyptus leaves, which have to be not only of a particular species but also of a certain age, because the older leaves contain prussic acid, which is toxic.

Large carnivores such as lions and tigers are used to eating almost their entire "kill" in the wild. Certainly scavengers and carrion feeders feed on the last remains of a carcass, but the carnivores consume flesh, entrails, liver, glands, brains, and the smaller bones. The bones are especially important for maintaining the animal's calcium content; without a regular intake of bone in its diet, the carnivore eventually suffers from spinal disorders. Zoo dieticians, therefore, make sure that the great cats receive enough of the type of bones that they can crush and swallow.

In recent years there has been a great development of huge aquariums, notably in Florida and California, for exhibiting the highly intelligent and entertaining dolphins and pilot whales. The Florida Marineland has actually succeeded in breeding pilot whales. These whales are small; the largest specimen, named Bimbo, was 18 feet long in 1962. Both dolphins and pilot whales are fish-eaters, but the aquariums are no more than watery cages, quite incapable of providing naturally the food chain of phytoplankton-zooplankton-small fish-large fish, and it is the last of these that is the food of toothed whales. These whales therefore have to be supplied with fish caught in the open sea; they are, in fact, just like any other caged animals, depending on man for a steady supply from outside.

This may seem obvious, but it has some bearing on the possibility of trying to breed some of the larger whales that are in danger of extinction, even if they could be trapped and confined. The whalebone whales, for example, are unusual because they skip the normal food chain and concentrate on plankton. The southern blue whale lives only on "krill," the collective name for millions of oceanic prawns (*Euphausia superba*) with an average length of 6 centimetres, and in the height of the antarctic summer probably consumes about 2 tons a day. Large shoals of krill are often to be seen from the crow's nest of a whale-catcher but the distribution of krill in antarctic waters is patchy, and it would take several ships working full time with plankton nets to keep one blue whale alive. Also the captive would have to be confined very close to the antarctic feeding grounds because dead krill rots quickly.

Above: A nine-year-old African elephant posing with his rations of food and water for one week (and keeper). The sacks on the left contain root vegetables and the bin on the right was full of colourful biscuits before the photography session. His food costs the London Zoo $3,000 per year.

Right: Zoos are always receiving for treatment domestic pets that have been badly cared for by their owners. This weeper capuchin monkey was brought in suffering from rickets, a deficiency disease caused by a shortage of vitamin D. On page 163 there is a picture of another of the higher primate suffering from a different deficiency disease. Turn to it now for a salutary comparison.

The almost insuperable problem of keeping such a whale alive is further complicated by the fact that southern blue whales feed only in the antarctic summer; their habit of life demands that in the winter they migrate up to 3000 miles into subtropical waters, where matings occur and young whales are born. In the winter months they eat almost nothing, and live on accumulated fat. Nobody knows what a blue whale would do if frustrated in its annual migrations, but clearly the larger whales cannot be bred in captivity.

Wild animals usually have a number of internal parasites that do them little harm in their natural environment but may, in captivity, respond to changes in the environment and diet of their host animal and become lethal to it. For instance, the okapi, which lives in the deep jungle of the Congo has to undergo a long course of de-worming before being exported, and on arrival at a zoo a further period of quarantine is necessary before it can safely be introduced to other okapis already in captivity.

The space problem already mentioned, has two different aspects. For instance, overcrowding in cages can lead to severe stress and fighting among animals constantly cooped up together. (We are learning a lot about overcrowding and its effect on humans from studying animals in zoos—p. 165). Also, in the days of small square cages, zoo keepers often wondered why many animals could not be induced to breed. One reason is that animals need exercise in order to keep healthy enough to breed. Another is that some birds, especially birds of prey, need to indulge in elaborate pre-mating display flights. Without the space for these special instinctive behaviour patterns, breeding will not take place. The Japanese white stork is being bred in captivity not because it is rare but because Japanese conservationists are becoming increasingly alarmed at the detrimental effect on these beautiful birds of the toxic chemicals used in agriculture. The interesting thing is that the storks are bred and reared in large "flight cages" where they can perform their mating ritual, and it is hoped that their offspring will be returned to the wild eventually, when the toxic chemicals have abated.

The importance of staff and zoo keepers is increasing as more and more is becoming known of the psychology of animals both in the wild and in captivity. Their relationship with humans is being given a good deal of attention, and it is no exaggeration to say that animals can take a positive like or dislike to their handlers. And not only do animals need to like their handlers, they also need (quite reasonably) to like their potential mates. It is simply no good putting a male and female together and expecting them to mate if their temperaments are incompatible. What is more, certain species may stick to one mate all their lives while others change about indiscriminately. Wolves, for instance, are very faithful; if a male wolf loses its mate it will hardly ever take another. In attempting to breed animals in captivity, zoo keepers must take this kind of thing into account.

Incidentally, there is an increased move among the larger zoos to specialize —that is, not to try to show specimens of every animal, but to limit their numbers and to set up collective or group exhibits. Although this is primarily an exhibition venture, it may well have a very fruitful by-product. As a group exhibit takes up more space and several species are grouped together, the natural habitat is more nearly reproduced than is possible with each species in isolation. One of these exhibits may be seen in the Bronx Zoo, New York. A variety of grazers and other herbivores are grouped together in an enclosure, and in the middle of the enclosure is an island, on which lions live. The lions are separated from their natural prey by a moat that runs all around the island. Thus no damage is done but both the public and the animals can see and feel something of the atmosphere of an African savannah. This will inevitably result in a more homely atmosphere and, we hope, in better breeding. Of course, there are always problems, even with captive animals that breed regularly. In the wild state, for example, where natural selection is in operation, the poorer individuals would not survive to maturity. It is thus of great importance that in a captive breeding stock the weaker progeny be ruthlessly weeded out.

Effects of Isolation   It is advisable to allow animals that have been in captivity for a long time to come into contact with an individual introduced into the group from the wild. This is because, without wild companions, caged individuals (of some, not all, species) not only do not breed but may even forget their natural habits. Not all behaviour is instinctive or innate; some of it is learnt from contact with other members of the same or even different species. The song of certain birds is a very good illustration of this. The wren, for example, seems to have an inborn knowledge of its own song, whereas the starling and the mocking-bird incorporates phrases from the songs of other species.

In the days when zoos, or even private animal breeders, kept a single example of a species in a cage together with a number of other birds, the incidence of imitative bird song was high. Nowadays, in the bigger zoos, birds are kept in pairs so that this happens less often. But when a foreign song has been learnt, a starling, for instance, is still able to pick up its own song very quickly if it hears another starling singing it.

Even the outward appearance, altered by selective breeding, will often revert back to that of the wild population after only a few generations. An interesting example of this is the budgerigar—a parakeet native to Australia. For a long time it has been very popular as a pet throughout Europe and the United States. Budgerigars often escape from their cages but usually they survive for only a short time in the wild before either they are eaten by a predator or they die of cold. In Florida, however, the climate is very similar to that of their native Australian habitat and those that have escaped are doing very well in the wild. There are an estimated 10,000 feral budgerigars in the forests of Florida, and these have made an interesting transition. Selective breeding had produced a wide variety of colours including blue, mauve, grey, and yellow, but the feral birds are quickly returning to their natural colouration—green with yellow heads.

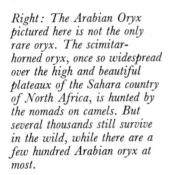

*Left Top: Australian budgerigars, the original wild type. Below: Some of the colours achieved by selective breeding in capitivity. **If budgerigars escape and become feral, recessive genes for blue or grey plumage are soon masked by the dominant genes for the green and yellow colouring of the original wild type.***

Right: The Arabian Oryx pictured here is not the only rare oryx. The scimitar-horned oryx, once so widespread over the high and beautiful plateaux of the Sahara country of North Africa, is hunted by the nomads on camels. But several thousands still survive in the wild, while there are a few hundred Arabian oryx at most.

"Doctor of the Arabs" Let us now take a close look at some examples of breeding in zoos. In some cases the animals concerned would not have survived in the wild, and in others they were—surprising as it may seem—already extinct.

One of the world's rarest and most attractive antelopes is the Arabian oryx. This beast was once very common and formerly lived over much of the Middle East. Since 1800 it has probably been restricted to the Arabian and Sinai peninsulas. Although its range was gradually reduced over the 19th and early 20th centuries, there was a disastrous change in the 1930s when the discovery of oil in the Middle East made the sheikhs extremely wealthy. With newly imported automobiles, the sheikhs began to hunt the Arabian oryx much more intensively. Sometimes they used as many as 300 automobiles in a single hunt, but the average was about 40; the rough, gravelly desert habitat of the oryx presented no problem for motor cars.

The oryx has always had a reputation among the Arabs for bravery, strength, and endurance, so it was not just wantonness that made the Arabs hunt them so pitilessly; they believed that by eating the meat of the oryx they would absorb some of its noble qualities. Indeed, one of the local names for the oryx is "Doctor of the Arabs."

Eventually, stocks of the Arabian oryx fell so low that a drive was mounted in 1962 by the British Fauna Preservation Society, assisted by the World

Wildlife Fund, to save it from extinction. An expedition was sent out to capture a small stock from an area east of Aden, in what is now the South Arabian Federation, and word was sent around asking if anyone knew of other possible sources. Word came back that 2 mangy specimens were wandering, apparently ownerless, in the soukh (market) of Taiz, capital of the Yemen. The expedition did not succeed in getting them (perhaps they were not as ownerless as they seemed to be) but Sheikh Jaber Abdulla al Sabah of Kuwait gave 3 beasts from his private herd. One of these survived the journey and joined an existing collection—2 males and 1 female—at the zoo at Phoenix in Arizona, where the climate was thought to be sufficiently like that of the Arabian peninsula. King Saud of Saudi Arabia presented 4 more.

By December 1967, there were 16 altogether, 9 males and 7 females. Oryxes take to captivity very well; they are docile and handle easily. This herd at Phoenix, another at Los Angeles, and at least two small captive herds in the Middle East, all augur well for the future of this animal, so recently one of the world's rarest animals. The Phoenix collection produced 5 calves between 1964 and 1966 and all the evidence shows that oryxes breed easily in captivity.

Breeding Back Another success story, also about an ungulate, starts in Mongolia. The plains near the Mongolian border with China are the home of one of the last true wild horses. This horse, named after its discoverer

It should be made clear from the start, that though the breeding-back experiments are not particularly valid scientifically, they are most interesting and amusing. Left—what they had to go on—the original tarpan painted by an unknown prehistoric artist on the wall of the Lascaux Caves, France. Right: What resulted—a tarpan, bred back from the closely related living Przewalski horse, at the Hellabrun Zoo, Munich.

Przewalski, is smaller than the domestic horse but its head is larger in proportion.

If this horse is to survive in its wild habitat there will have to be co-operation between the governments of the Chinese and Mongolian People's Republics although, as a matter of fact, neither the Mongolian nor the Chinese nomadic herdsmen go there very much nowadays. Because of improved methods of animal husbandry there is no need for the nomads to wander so far in search of pasture. The Przewalski horse is, none the less, rare in the wild, but there have been numerous sightings in the past year. Since interest in this wild horse was aroused at the end of the last century, expeditions have been sent out to the Mongolian plains. From 1899 to 1907 twelve specimens were brought back, but only 3 survived to maturity.

Between 1925 and 1935 four more were transported from Russia to Germany (with a permit) and then 2 more (without a permit). There the breeding experiments with the Przewalski horse began. It was long thought that the Mongolian form was very closely related to a European wild horse known as the *tarpan*. The tarpan figures in many prehistoric cave paintings but it became extinct only recently; the last one died in captivity in 1919. The theory was that a large part of the genetical make-up of the tarpan still survived in the Asiatic Przewalski race of the same species; it was believed that some tarpan qualities survived in the domestic horse but that they had become diluted through selective breeding. It was on this basis that the

Przewalski horses (above) are the last of the true wild horses. There are however many varieties of true wild asses in Asia and Africa. But the Indian form is shot for the supposed aphrodisiac qualities of its testes; the Persian form because its bile is thought to cure cataract of the eye. At this rate it cannot be long before the wild asses suffer the same fate as the wild horses.

Heck brothers of the Munich and Berlin zoos started their experiments to breed back the tarpan. By 1967 there were 10 specimens (8 females and 2 males) of the so-called bred-back tarpan in the Hellabrunn zoo at Munich.

Meanwhile, efforts continued, mainly at the Prague zoo, to increase the numbers of the pure-bred Przewalski horse. By January 1967, there were 146 in captivity altogether and a system of keeping stud-books had proved very successful. These stud-books were set out with a complete page for each individual, listing its name and full details of its parentage. For example, one specimen, born in Munich in 1943 and sent to the Russian Askaniya-Nova zoo in 1948, appears twice in the stud-books; in its original entry it is known as Robert but the Russians changed its name to Orlik so that it is now registered in the stud-book as Robert-Orlik. Orlik was used for 10 years as a breeder. Another specimen is now no longer used for breeding; the stud-book states that it has a white blaze on its forehead, which is a sign that it has too much domestic horse in its genetical make-up.

Ancestral cattle The gene pool was used by the Heck brothers to even greater effect to breed back another animal, which had been extinct since 1627. In theory at least, every creature has in its genetical make-up some of the characteristics possessed by its ancestors; each one of us, for instance, has half those of our mother and half those of our father. This means that we are composed of a quarter of each of our grandparents, one eighth of our great-grandparents, and so on. Of course, it is not as simple as that, because genetically controlled characteristics operate by passing on one of two alternative characteristics from each parent. This is why you may have red

Top left: Paintings from the Lascaux caves such as this one gave the only direct clues about the colour of the aurochs. The other physical features were discernible from a few engravings, one of Magdalenian age, carved on a stalagmite; another based on the last surviving specimen. Some of the domestic breeds used in breeding back the aurochs are shown centre left to far right; Scottish, Alpine, and Hungarian. Right: Aurochsen bred back by Heinz Heck of the Munich Zoo.

hair when neither of your parents has it. One of them may have a gene for red hair masked by one for brown; it is a matter of chance which gene you receive.

The Heck brothers decided that within the genetical make-up of all the world's domestic cattle must be the complete formula for the long-extinct aurochs—the form from which all today's stocks were originally bred. They set about proving it. It was difficult because the appearance of the aurochs was known only from a few pictures. It was known to have longer legs and bigger horns and to be as large as or larger than the biggest cattle of today. It was black with a yellowish-white stripe along its back, and grew a shaggy winter coat, shedding it for a smooth coat in the summer. The Heck brothers also studied ancient Egyptian frescoes of the Mediterranean breed, to get as much background information as possible.

Around 1921 Heinz Heck began by taking one breed with the right sort of horns and breeding it with another of the right sort of colour. He saved a lot of time by using some ready made hybrids too, and success came quickly. By 1932 he produced the first new aurochs. Even more curious and interesting was that the calf was brown, as in the original description, and developed the stripe as it grew older. (The American bison and another bovid, the Indian wild ox called the *gaur*, also have brown calves that change colour later.) The original aurochs was known to have certain mental characteristics and some of these mental properties returned with the breeding; like the original aurochs they were ferocious and short-tempered in captivity but, when returned to the wild, Heinz Heck's aurochsen were wary and shy and hid themselves deep in the woodland. When his brother Lutz Heck tried a similar experiment but using different crosses for his breeding, he came up with an animal extraordinarily similar to the others. The aurochs is also quite immune to the usual diseases of cattle, so there may possibly be a practical outcome to this fascinating series of experiments.

The experiments of Heinz Heck did not stop there; he knew that our own horse is descended from a wild form that may originally have been striped. The various kinds of zebras show several stages of stripe loss. For instance the quagga (extinct in 1870s) had stripes only on its front quarters. It was, as you might say, giving up stripes. Heck was having considerable success breeding back the quagga from zebras by selecting the less completely striped off-spring, but World War II interrupted his experiment. The question we have to ask ourselves about breeding back is: how can we know whether the whole formula of an extinct animal has been reassembled? We can judge only by external characteristics and by a few records of temperament, about which we can know little. This does not detract from the interest of the Heck brothers' experiments, but we must be wary of accepting that an extinct animal has been "brought back to life" in all respects.

Infertile Tortoises   As it is preferable to try to breed endangered species before, rather than after, they become extinct, the San Diego and other zoos undertook the task of breeding the Galapagos giant tortoise. These creatures have always been infrequent breeders, even in the days when they were being plundered from the islands. Zoo experts had no false hopes that once in captivity the tortoise would step up its breeding rate. Even so, the early experiments were not very successful. Collection for establishing a breeding stock started in the late 1920s and originally colonies were set up at several zoos.

The first successful hatchings were in Bermuda in 1939, where 5 eggs hatched out of 8; meanwhile the San Diego colony produced nothing. There were about 20 specimens there in the early 1930s, and from time to time more tortoises were brought in from the Galapagos islands. The larger colony should have had a higher fertility rate than before, but the early batches of eggs proved to be infertile.

Eventually it occurred to the curator of reptiles that what was lacking was a suitable area for copulation. The floor of the pen was made of a rather compact and unyielding earth; the curator thought that possibly the male could not get into the proper position on a hard floor, (though it seems more likely that the female was unable to dig her nest). So in 1957 the San Diego zoo modified the enclosure and put down an entirely new floor of soft river sand. Soon afterwards, one of the females laid a batch of eggs. Nesting among tortoises is quite complicated. It begins with a close examination of the sandy enclosure by the female; she wanders about and stops frequently to smell the sand. When she has selected a site, she starts to excavate, squirting urine on to the nest area to moisten the sand. The nest, which she digs with her hind legs, is jug-shaped—that is, wider at the bottom than at the top. The eggs are white and spherical and an average clutch is between 10 and 20. One female at San Diego produced 153 eggs over 6 years and another has laid about 110; so it is not the lack of eggs that has caused the poor hatching results. One possible reason is that the eggs are laid from a height and some are cracked in the process. Not content with this, the female rolls the eggs about within the nest, and this almost inevitably cracks a few more.

When she has finished laying she covers the eggs with sand and stamps it down vigorously. More eggs may be cracked at this stage. Despite this rather wasteful process, about which the zoo can do nothing, there has been a great increase in the numbers of young born alive. The natural incubation period is not known for certain, because the keepers remove the eggs from the nest and place them in large crocks in heated rooms with minimum temperatures of about 90°F. The first batch, in 1961, was incubated at about 80°F, and after 173 days the first young tortoise to hatch had worked its way out of its egg and up to the sandy surface of the crock, where it was found waddling about, to the delight of the keepers. Although the San Diego colony, as well as other smaller ones in Bermuda and Honolulu, are now breeding successfully, fertility remains generally low (6.98 per cent out of 257 eggs producing live young at San Diego). As no other reason can be found, the conclusion that the zoo authorities draw from this is that even in the wild, Galapagos giant tortoises have always produced a great many eggs that never hatched.

Breeding of rare animals, especially those that need a lot of space, is not exclusive to city zoos. There are private collections such as the one already mentioned at Woburn Abbey, owned by the Duke of Bedford. This collection is very varied and includes rheas, various bison, and the Manchurian sika deer. But the undisputed pride of the collection is the now famous herd of deer known as Père David's deer after Père Armand David, who discovered them in rather extraordinary circumstances: the mi-lu—as this deer was called in its native China—has been extinct in the wild for many thousands of years. One herd was kept in captivity, however, in the Peking hunting park for the delectation of the Imperial Court.

When Armand David visited the park in the late 1800s, he saw the deer and had no doubt that it was a species unknown to western science. He arranged for some to be shipped out to the Paris and Berlin zoos, where the first breeding herds were established. It is fortunate that he did so, because very few of the original herd survived. Opinion varies as to what happened: one authority states that floods swept through Peking and the wall of the park was breached. All but a few of the deer escaped and were either drowned or eaten by starving peasants (who could hardly be expected to distinguish a rare species from a common one). The other authority maintains that the wall was breached during a political insurrection (with the same result). The

Left : Vertical series shows the Galapagos tortoise laying her eggs in a pit, the eggs themselves, and a newly hatched tortoise. These pictures are of giant tortoises kept and bred in captivity at the San Diego Zoo. Above : S. American maned wolf, rare and declining. A brew made from its bone shavings is given to pregnant women and said to ease delivery. It has been successfully bred in Frankfurt Zoo ; this beautiful wolf, which would soon be hunted to extinction, has been rescued by captivity.

Woburn herd now numbers 400 and there are another 100 dispersed in other public and private zoos.

Our last example of captive breeding is that of the golden hamster—a pretty little rodent, and a very popular pet. What most people do not realize is that every single golden hamster alive today is descended from a single pregnant female found in Syria in 1920. Despite numerous collecting trips to the original area, no other golden hamster has ever been found. It cannot now be considered rare, although it is apparently extinct in the wild; on the contrary it is very prolific and, though the mother tends to eat her young if disturbed, hamsters are otherwise easy to keep and breed well in captivity.

Many of the animals we have talked about in these chapters can be seen in zoos in the larger cities. In most zoos there is a good system of labelling exhibits, and if a species is rare there is a notice to this effect, together with a map of its present range and perhaps some information about its diet and habits in the wild. This is the only chance that most of us get to see some of these animals so it is well worth the visit. But conservationists realize that zoos are not the ideal answer to the problem of preserving rare species. It is important not only to preserve a species in isolation in a zoo, but, if possible, to preserve the habitat as well. This is perhaps the biggest part of nature conservation, as we shall see in the next chapter.

Javan tiger (above) and Goeldi's tamarin (right) are two more animals that will probably be extinct in the wild before long, but they have been saved by being bred in captivity. Javan tigers decline in numbers even though the locals believe they are reincarnate souls of their ancestors. Four have been bred in various zoos; this one is in Budapest. The tamarins are being sold as pets, but they need special care if they are to breed in captivity. They have a limited range in Brazil and Peru.

Before animals become so rare that recovery becomes impossible, conservationists try to keep an eye on numbers; perhaps by marking individual animals or by removing them to an area of greater safety, as is being done with this polar bear.

CHAPTER 6

RESERVES – A REPRIEVE FOR NATURE

Conservationists tend to be idealists who care about the natural world and would like to see some of it salvaged from the harmful influence of man. When this means demanding that legal protection be given to rare species, their job is difficult enough; when it means demanding that land should be set aside to safeguard a remnant of the natural world, conservationists are up against both ideological and economic opposition—as we shall see.

So far the conservation movement has had a comparatively small measure of success; only a fraction of the Earth's surface that is available has been bought by Nature Trusts, or appropriated by national or local governments to be administered as reserves.

Reserves can be designated for many purposes: for preserving a particular type of habitat; for the protection of vegetation or of animals in their natural environment; for scientific research; and—implicit in the ideals of the National Park type of reserve—for the education, enjoyment, and recreation of the public. Many reserves and parks can also become an economic asset, but it is notoriously difficult to persuade most governments that it is worth while setting aside land for conservation. The public, too, are oblivious of the complexities of putting conservation ideals into practice but they are certainly willing to use the amenities of National Parks once they are provided.

A reserve can be the size of a small pond or millions of acres in area. There are wildlife reserves such as the Gir Forest in India, areas of magnificent and spectacular scenery such as the Engadine National Park in Switzerland, swamps teeming with crocodiles such as the Florida Everglades, lakes and rivers for fishing and boating, steep mountains for hiking and skiing, extinct volcanoes such as the Ngorongoro crater in Tanzania, as well as live volcanoes in many parts of South America. There are also smaller reserves, such as the Mosi-oa-Tunya, which means "the smoke that thunders," in Lozi (these famous falls were for a time known as the Victoria Falls but reverted to the original name after Zambia gained independence). There are famous buildings, religious shrines, archaeological and anthropological remains—for example, the strange sculptured heads of Easter Island, and aboriginal cave paintings in Australia. There are geological phenomena such as the immense Grand Canyon, and deserts and valleys carved out by glaciers. There is the Cerro de Comanche National Park in Bolivia, devoted to the protection of a flower that blooms regularly every 125 years, and a minute reserve in the middle of the Negev Desert in Israel that protects a cluster of breathtakingly beautiful irises. In short there is an astonishing variety of different types of scenery, habitat, and natural phenomenon that have been designated as reserves and National Parks. Their names can be confusing, however; a reserve can be called anything from a sanctuary, a refuge, a game park, or a game reserve, to a National Park or a National Monument. Some are quite private and devoted to research only, others are open to the public; some are within built-up areas, others are all but inaccessible.

All have one thing in common: the land has been put aside from the mainstream of urban and rural planning for some special purpose. Reserves are so many and so varied that it is impossible to be comprehensive, so we shall try to look at some widely different types of conservation areas—beginning as usual with some of the problems involved.

When a reserve is set aside, an embargo is put on human settlements within the area if possible, and where settlements already exist, further growth may be prohibited; every effort is made to keep the area stable in accordance with ecological laws. But is this practicable, or merely an ideal?

When an area is set aside as a reserve, the ecological balance is disturbed as surely as if the whole had been surrounded by a wall. As we know from

Chapter 2, nature is not static; an ecosystem is in a perpetual state of flux: plants, animals, soil, and atmosphere are in constant interaction. To set an artificial boundary on these interacting processes upsets the equilibrium around the edges. Gradually, depending on the size of the reserve, the subtle changes in ecological processes will filter inward and ultimately affect the whole reserve. The larger a reserve is, the longer this encroachment will take and the greater the chance of the whole being self-supporting. In a small reserve not only is interaction with the outside more severe, but the habitat is more vulnerable to disease and to human interference.

In the case of wetland and marshland reserves, a small area is useless unless there is some guarantee that the water table, which determines the environment, remains stable. This seldom happens, because drainage or some other development in the surrounding country, even quite a distance away, can easily upset the water level.

Islands can be turned into sanctuaries with smaller danger of interference than a land-locked reserve. But even with an island there are risks. Uncontrolled fishing, or pollution of the surrounding waters can affect the littoral zone (the sea-shore) and this rather specialized habitat is in contact with the food webs of the interior; thus damage can occur even if people do not go ashore complete with rats, dogs, and diseases.

We mentioned the encroachment of outside influences *into* reserves; the opposite situation also exists where it is difficult to prevent the ecosystem

Far Left: The Pasque flower of Gloucestershire, England is rare, and fast disappearing from its limestone habitat. Conservation of wild flowers in Britain is often the concern of vigilant local communities who enforce the protection of rare species. Near left: All wild flowers are protected in the Swiss National Parks. Gentians (the purple flower shown here) are, however, picked for making liqueurs.

Right: A gannet and guillemot sanctuary at Sula Sgeir Island off the Outer Hebrides. This species of gannet is confined to the north Atlantic and the rock, a sub-oceanic island, is the only British gannetry on which numbers seem to be decreasing.

inside reserves from spreading outward. Even in the largest inland reserves, to contain the ecosystem indefinitely presents great problems. Migrating birds cannot, of course, be contained all the year round in a reserve, but even lions, for instance, wander away from the Nairobi Park into the city's suburbs, and walk around sedately before returning to the park where—apart from occasional fits of boredom—they seem very contented.

Many grazing animals need to cover large distances in search of food. If they do not have a very specific diet, the problem is less acute. But if animals graze only one type of plant they tend to follow in the wake of their food as it establishes itself in new areas. The development of a plant succession can be in a mosaic (filling in empty spaces) and also in an advancing "front." If the front advances outside the boundaries of the reserve, it becomes impossible to contain primary consumers that feed on it. The conservationist is then faced with two alternatives. One is to allow the reserve to run itself, and to remain ecologically intact while running the risk of dissipation at the borders and some loss of game. The other is to try to prevent undue losses, by imposing man-made judgments and thus destroying the natural balance to some extent. This dilemma causes one of the most basic conflicts in the theory of conservation. We shall see how the two schools of thought can affect policy in the management of reserves.

Drought So far we have mentioned only certain problems that arise in normal conditions. But what happens to a reserve in extreme conditions, when the balance of nature is seriously disturbed? During a period of drought many animals will die; others will go miles in search of water. Water birds and amphibians will search for new lakes or ponds, and a great deal of pressure will be put on the water sources that are left.

During a drought several years ago in the Tsavo Royal Park in Kenya, rhino were dying at a rate of three a day; but a herd of elephants trekked 30 miles to reach water. Elephants can get water from dried-up river beds by excavating a hole with their front feet and blowing the sandy water off the surface with their trunks; then they can drink from the clearer water below. As the average intake is 38 gallons, it is quite a problem for an elephant to slake its thirst. But it has a better chance of survival than human beings; during a drought in the Tsavo Park a group of visitors was found after nine days just as its members were preparing to commit suicide.

Several game reserves in Africa have collected money to provide boreholes, windmills, and drinking tanks. The whole installation can cost well over $10,000, and it must be well protected (by fences made from old railway track) against attack by elephants. If the water in the drinking tank is used up elephants become enraged and easily destroy windmill, tower, tank, and all. Lack of money limits the number of boreholes and windmills but some game parks—such as the Albert Park, in the Congo, for instance—do not permit any interference with the ecological balance, and to provide extra water certainly amounts to interference. The Albert Park policy is based on the fact that drought results in competition for water, which in turn results in natural selection of those animals that can survive on less. The long-term advantage of this selection will be seen in the differences in water requirements between domestic cattle and, say, the eland antelope (p. 174).

Food Shortage Even during periods of comparatively stable conditions, overgrazing in a game park or nature reserve is always a problem. Overgrazed land always takes time to recover and an occasional drought invariably aggravates the situation. The question here is whether to provide extra food and salt licks or to leave well alone. The privately owned land surrounding a reserve is often very tempting to wild life—especially when food is short. There are many tales of deer wandering even into suburbs and nibbling at neatly trimmed hedges and shrubberies, and of small animals raiding dustbins. This generates yet another conflict—between those who are responsible for the reserve and those who live outside it.

At one time in the Addo Park in the Cape Province of South Africa, elephants took to roaming on to the neighbouring land and stealing oranges and grapefruit from the citrus farms. As a counter-measure, the farmers dumped fruit that was unsalable into the reserve so that the elephants would not stray. But the elephants still preferred fresh fruit, and went on invading the orchards. The farmers then put an electric fence around the boundary, but the elephants soon got used to the shocks, so that after about a year it was no longer effective. To raise the voltage would have endangered human lives, so, once again, old railway track proved an effective barrier.

Fires In many parts of the world, bush fires cause a tremendous amount of damage. Often these fires are started deliberately to stimulate the growth of new grass by burning off the dead grass cover. But although controlled firing benefits pasture used solely for grazing, a fire in open grasslands often gets out of control and spreads very rapidly. If a bush fire spreads into a nature reserve it causes an ecological disaster. Most of the vegetation recovers fairly quickly, but the destruction of the ground cover means that the larger animals fleeing in panic from the advancing flames have to go somewhere and they may then overcrowd another area. Also there are smaller creatures (rodents, snakes, worms, bacteria, spiders, and so on) that make their homes in logs, under bushes, in holes in the ground, or in the soil itself. Although less conspicuous they are as much and as vital a part of the whole ecosystem as the larger herbivores and carnivores. This devastated land has to be recolonized and gradually restored to the stage at which it can support a balanced complement of consumers.

Disease Wild game animals, especially in the tropics, are storehouses of disease. Many tropical diseases are caused by parasites carried by mammals and spread by insects. There have been many concerted attempts at stamping out this type of disease, and vast numbers of game animals have been slaughtered in an attempt to exterminate the parasites. To leave pockets of carriers in nature reserves must surely negate much of the effort. Control of pests and tropical diseases is a vast subject on its own and we shall say more about it in Chapter 8. The question here is whether any type of disease control, whether slaughter or immunization, is ecologically sound in a reserve: in Chapter 3 we suggested that endemic disease could be viewed as a mechanism of natural selection. This is the stand that the "leave the ecosystem alone" school must take if they are to be consistent.

Research Reserves that provide facilities for research are very valuable to the biologist and ecologist because an area that is kept as natural as possible forms an ideal outdoor laboratory. Administrators of reserves are called upon to provide certain facilities for visiting scientists. They are asked to build up as complete a collection as possible of all the plants and animals to be found in the area. Special importance is attached to soil organisms, disease carriers, the ecologically predominant types of insects, molluscs, and spiders, as well as the larger land and water animals, trees, shrubs, and other plants. This provides what is known as a *comparative collection* and aids the scientist in identifying any specimen he may collect in the area. In addition to the main collection, field identification manuals should be provided, such as the excellent guide to the trees and shrubs of the Kruger National Park. These are useful both to research workers and to tourists.

Above: In the Kalahari Gemsbok Park, windmills are vital; the rivers flow only about twice a century. Above right: Elephant drinking from a tank in the Murchison Falls Park, Uganda. This Park is really spectacular and famous for its elephant herds.

Right: "Desolation Trail" in Hawaii's National Park. The Park is famous for its active volcanoes and for its endemic wildlife. The Hawaiian goose, once exterminated from its native home has been reintroduced after captive breeding in the USA.

The administrators and game wardens undertake systematic surveys that are carried out both by means of aerial photographs and by observation on the ground. Detailed soil maps are compiled and vegetation distribution of the area plotted, as well as detailed topographical maps and large-scale geological survey maps. Meteorological stations are being set up—in the larger reserves, at least. With this background information it is then possible to plot changing factors such as the quantity of food consumed in different areas and the natural fluctuations of ecologically dominant animals. Plotting of fertility and breeding rates and the rate of turnover from one generation to the next is carried out by a process called "marking." A proportion of animals are captured and marked with coded colours so that their subsequent movements can be plotted. Game marking is done on the same principle as the ringing of migratory birds; ringed birds may be picked up thousands of miles away but game marking helps to study movements and feeding routes within the reserves. Once birds are ringed, the public is asked to co-operate in sending the details required (shown in the information on the tag) back to the research station. With game surveys, too, the public can be roped in to help once the animals are marked. One such, nicknamed "Operation Necktie," was carried out in the Kruger National Park in order to find out more about the grazing movements of zebra in the park. The organizer of the project immobilized a proportion of the zebra population by drugs, and tied around their necks 12 different patterns of tie. An antidote to the immobilizing drug was then administered; when the zebras had recovered sufficiently, they were spanked into action and they got up and trotted away suffering no ill effects. The antidote is important because, without it, the animals could so easily become victims of a predator while still in a dazed condition. Visitors to the park were then given a questionnaire that they were asked to complete by stating which patterns of tie they saw in different parts of the park. In this way a great deal of useful work was done at no more cost than that of the neckties.

Game counting is also done by a process known as *telemetry* (measuring from a distance). At first only large animals such as giraffes and elephants were counted this way but the technique is being extended to smaller beasts such as rabbits. Telemetry consists of immobilizing the animal and fixing a battery-driven radio transmitter onto its body. This transmitter then emits signals that can be picked up on a directional receiver at the research station; the movement of the marked game can then be plotted easily until the battery runs down, which may take several weeks.

Much of the biological research done nowadays does not rely only on observation at a distance; experiments are also needed for verification of theories. For instance, one project, carried out on zebras in the Nairobi National Park, was aimed at measuring the temperature directly below the skin, by inserting thermometers—again using immobilizing drugs. The researchers confirmed that the temperature below the black stripes is higher than that below the white stripes; it was already known that black absorbs more heat than white, so that these results were really rather to be expected.

Researchers also take full advantage of the regular game-cropping programmes. Everyone is alerted when cropping is about to begin and anyone interested in a portion of the animal in question comes along. As soon as the beast is killed, it is dissected and carved up; some take specimens from the liver, pancreas, stomach lining, and so on; others take blood samples; almost every part of the animal is utilized, including the muscle (meat), which is carved up and distributed among the helpers and sold to nearby villages.

Once back at the laboratory, the researchers fix and mount the tissue samples on microscope slides for detailed study, not only for their own use, but to send to scientists all over the world who are studying similar problems elsewhere. Only if a biologist demands the killing of particularly rare animals for research purposes is there likely to be friction with the game wardens. Usually they work together with the researchers very amicably.

Game wardens tend to be reluctant to upset the ecological balance of the reserve by interfering with animals or plants simply for experiments. But research is needed to understand in more detail the effects of disease, fire, chemical pesticides, and so on, and this involves collecting and often killing specimens. The researchers maintain, with good reason, that these enquiries should be carried out on the spot—under the guidance of ecologists, and indeed the game wardens themselves, who are well acquainted with local conditions—rather than thousands of miles away in a laboratory, working on preserved, rather than fresh, material. And although most parks do not have research laboratories in the very heart of the reserve, the nearer the work is done to the actual area concerned, the better.

Zoning One of the aims of conservation is to make the best possible use of land, and this ideal can well be applied to reserves by setting up a system of zoning. Under this system an inner zone remains inviolate, untouched by researchers or visitors. This zone acts as a reservoir—in fact as a "gene bank" —providing new genetic material for the rest of the reserve. Other areas are zoned according to function: In one, research is permitted; in another, visitors can move freely on foot; in yet another, there are roads for motor traffic; and so on. In this way, a single reserve could function successfully for a number of different purposes.

Most of the research carried out within reserves is on what is known as "pure" ecology, though some of it may be in "applied" ecology, in which the results of research are applied to industry, forestry, or wild life management. A good example of pure research is the work that is being done on the establishment of primary and secondary plant successions on newly cooled lava such as exists on the Virunga volcanoes in the Congo Albert Park. Applied research, on the other hand, can be of national importance. Argentina, for example, exports a material useful for tanning leather, extracted from the heartwood of the quebracho tree. In order to determine future policy, it was vital to know how long this tree takes to regenerate. It

Left page : A Kob antelope, immobilized and marked (above). After it is set free, its movements will then be traced by game wardens. Below left : One of the marked animals has been eaten by a lion. Its coding enables the wardens to trace the average life span and pattern of movement in the reserve. Below right : A royal tern is marked by ringing so that its subsequent movements can be recorded.

Right page : The rare Cape mountain zebra (above left), immobilized by drug-darting, being measured before it is set free again. Below left : Lions in the Amboseli National Park, watched by research workers from a camouflaged vehicle. Above right : Cropping hippos to keep numbers down. The operation is carried out strictly according to the game warden's calculations. Centre right : Every part of a cropped animal is used for food, or research. A foetus has been dissected out of an elephant that has been cropped. It will be preserved and kept in the reserve's collection for study. Below right : Loading a crated Hunter's antelope into a helicopter in one of Kenya's big reserves. Helicopters are invaluable in game management.

Left: Buffalo, again plentiful in the west, being rounded up by cowboys and translocated (in the broadest sense) to be sold for meat. This wild herd is, in fact, being cropped to keep the numbers of buffalo constant.

Above right: White rhino in the Madi district of Uganda, about to be captured and translocated to Murchison Falls Park. Below: As the waters of Kariba rise, an immobilized rhino is strapped to a barge for removal to safety.

grows in two reserves—the Pilcomayo and Chaco National Parks; but unfortunately the designation of these parks in 1951 and 1954 respectively did not halt grazing and other interference sufficiently for the park to be used for this research, and it had to be carried out at great additional expense in especially created research stations. This shows the importance of zoning for research, and the difficulty of enforcing protection laws even in important National Parks. Even in a zone set aside for research, one worker can disturb another sometimes with comical results. In one instance an ornithological study in the Amazon rain-forest overlapped with a forestry research project. The bird watcher had cleared a few inconspicuous trails in the forest to allow him to creep about noiselessly. The forestry workers found the trails invaluable for spotting plant specimens and felled several trees, thereby destroying the habitats of the birds under observation. It is on record that the ornithologist later forgave the botanists, who published some very important results from the field-work they had done in the forest.

From surveys and research projects carried out by field ecologists and the resident staff, information is collected and pooled; this helps in policy making and management. If the reserve is one that allows some interference with nature, the staff not only construct wind pumps, provide salt licks, stop bush fires, combat disease outbreaks, mend broken legs, and hand-rear young, but also put the results of the various game surveys to good use.

Wildlife Management One of the biggest tasks is the regulation of the predator-prey-pasture balance as far as possible and to do this it may be necessary to transfer animals from areas where pressure on food is high to other areas where it is lower. They do this either in the way cowboys drive cattle or by a technique known as *translocation*.

In its broadest sense translocation merely means moving animals (or anything else) from one place to another. In the sense it is used here, years of research and experiment have gone into perfecting its techniques, and it has

revolutionized large-scale game management. First, for translocation to be successful there must be a detailed understanding of the ecological and physiological requirements of the animals to be moved. Second, removing animals from place to place can involve them in a good deal of trauma and it is this problem that has been so successfully solved by a new technique known as drug-darting. This was first used on a big scale from 1959–1963 during the construction of the Kariba Dam on the Zambezi River. As the waters of the lake rose, animals were left stranded on rapidly shrinking islands; the rescue operation was dubbed "Operation Noah" and its purpose was to remove large numbers of animals from these islands to the mainland and there to set them free or to translocate them to a reserve. Drug darting techniques are also used frequently in game marking; it saves chasing animals to exhaustion, which could result in reducing their chance of survival and thus spoil the survey. Although the technique is used on many different kinds of animals, and for many different purposes, it has been particularly successful in translocating dangerous and bulky rhinos.

First, the rhino is approached by jeep or on foot, and injected—not by hand, but by a dart (loaded with a tranquilizing drug) fired from a crossbow or a gun. The drug's purpose is to make the rhino docile without actually anaesthetizing it. A fully unconscious rhino presents problems—because of its great weight it may break its bones as it falls, or even die from asphyxiation because of the pressure of its own weight on its lungs.

Several different kinds of drugs have been tried and it has been found that tranquilizers mixed with synthetic morphine make a rhino docile. Onlookers watch with astonishment as a full-grown rhinoceros is passively led by one man and persuaded to enter a travelling crate.

Translocation experiments since "Operation Noah" have been most successful and techniques have been improved so much that very few animals die in the process. In Zululand, in the Umfolozi reserve, white rhinos particularly have been bred and redistributed to other parts of Africa where stocks had become depleted. Since 1962 Rhodesia has received white rhinoceroses from Umfolozi, and the restocking of other areas with both black and white rhinos is proceeding along similar lines; specimens have also been sent to zoos all over the world. As a result of the efficient and timely conservation of the Umfolozi white rhino, this animal, once listed in the *Red Data Book* as being in the utmost danger of extinction, is well on the way to being saved for posterity.

While on the subject of rhinos, it is worth talking about the Asian forms, which *are* in very great danger. The largest of the Asian forms is the Great Indian rhinoceros; this beast, which has deep body folds, may reach a length of 14 feet and carries a horn that may be 2 feet in length. The range of this rhino is confined to six reserves in India and the Rapti Valley of Nepal. The most severely endangered forms, however, are the Javan and Sumatran rhinos. The Javan rhino looks like the Indian form in that it also has deeply etched body folds that give a somewhat armour-plated look. There may be

The Oka National Park is one of Russia's smaller reserves. It is set in forests and marshes and it gives protection to a variety of animals and plants. Right: A food rack for deer. Below left: The rare European bison, now extinct in the wild. Below right: A beaver dam.

no more than between 25 and 40 Javan rhinos left alive and they are not breeding fast enough to ensure the survival of another generation. These are confined to the Udjong Kulon reserve in western Java, but there is also a small area on the Thailand frontier that seems to contain a few, to judge from the occasional sale of horns in this region.

The Sumatran rhino is the smallest species and, in early life at least, is covered with short hair. This rhino is protected over only a part of its range— in the Löser reserve in Sumatra. Unfortunately, although it is protected by law, in Burma it is still legal to sell rhino blood for medicinal purposes.

We described translocation in terms of the most difficult animal to handle but it must be realized that not all animals redistributed in this way are large brutes. Translocation is helping to save other, smaller threatened species. We have said that the lemurs of Malagasy are being very badly hit by the destruction of the forest. As it seems clear that setting a sanctuary aside on Malagasy itself is not going to provide adequate protection, the small island of Nossi Mangabey, where some of the east-coast forest is still relatively intact, has been set aside as a lemur sanctuary. A few different kinds of lemur have been translocated to Nossi Mangabey where the habitat can support them.

Russian National Parks do a good deal of work in re-introducing animals into areas from which they have become reduced or extinct. The sable, the musk-rat, various ungulates, and birds are often translocated to new areas tens or hundreds of kilometres from the reserves in which they were reared. Beavers, too, are trapped and translocated from the Voronezh, the Berezin and many other reserves, with the result that there are now an estimated 10,000 beavers in the USSR, where quite recently they were practically extinct. Most of the translocation done in the USSR, however, is for the restocking of hunting grounds. In New South Wales, Australia, over 7000 young koalas were translocated to restock areas such as Mount Kosciusko State Park where their numbers had become drastically reduced.

For a great many tasks in a large reserve, aeroplanes are invaluable; where finance is not too limited, they are being used more and more. In translocation, or in rescuing sick or trapped animals, for instance, one pilot can direct his staff on the ground straight to the spot, provide medicines and any supplies that may be needed, and ferry small animals to safety. Aerial game-counts are also made from aeroplanes as well as surveys of damage by fires, flooding, or overgrazing—of damage done to trees by elephants, and so on.

Ethics of Poaching   One of the principal uses of the aeroplane in game reserves is for enforcement of the park's regulations, and this means detecting poachers and their caches of ivory, skins, rhino horn, biltong, and so on. The Tsavo Royal National Park was recently equipped with an aeroplane, and the game wardens soon found dumps of poached elephant ivory that were worth enough to pay for the running costs of the plane for the first year. Conservationists denounce poaching and poachers so universally that it is perhaps worth taking a closer look at the problem so as to see both viewpoints.

The *Red Data Book* is full of dismal reports of the effects of uncontrollable poaching; we have already talked about them in relation to rhinos, alligators, and others in Chapter 4. There is, for instance, an example of the protection conferred on a particularly rare mountain goat, the serow of Taiwan. This goat was rigidly protected under the Japanese occupation, but after World war II the law lapsed and, although it was re-enacted in 1948, it has never been enforced. "In addition," the report goes on to say, "the mountain-dwelling aborigines are in fact issued with hunting permits and free ammunition." The priorities of that conservationist are clear; he is for the survival of the serow. But hunting is the way of life of the aborigines, as it is with many peoples all over the world. To these peoples, conservation laws are irrelevant when pitted against their own needs for survival. Unfortunately for those who live in and near reserves, hunting changes its name to poaching. They are told that hunting is forbidden in the game reserves—forbidden, that is, to those without a permit; and to shoot game without a permit is an offence punishable by fine or imprisonment. The question is, can everyone get a permit? This is not always easy to answer. Take East Africa, for example, where in principle anyone can get a permit, but in practice the price is so high that the local tribesmen cannot afford it. Permits are issued on demand to hunters and the so-called hunting tourists, however, because the permit system is in fact a method of earning foreign currency. This practice is defended by many game-park administrators, who say that the hunters operate under strict supervision (after paying a considerable fee, which is put to good use) and are permitted to shoot only a specific quota of the wild life. Indeed they receive cards with details of the game they are and are not allowed to shoot, according to game surveys carried out regularly by the game wardens. This is certainly regulation of game according to strict rules of conservation, but is it ethical? How does one convince an African that it is fair for him to go to prison for a year for "poaching" while someone else is alowed to "hunt." Hunting for sport has always been the preserve of the privileged. Most people in Europe, for example, cannot afford to buy fishing rights on rivers or to rent a well-stocked pheasant shoot for a season, and those who cannot afford to hunt go out at night and try their luck if the urge or the need is great enough. In Europe, however, most people are not so deficient in protein as they once were, and hunting is anyway no longer the traditional way of life. But in many underdeveloped countries, the dubious advantages of industrialization and supermarkets have not yet replaced hunting as a source of food, and so, until the people are given a viable alternative, hunting is bound to continue. The profit motive almost always determines the attitude of land owners, and nature reserves are less profitable than farms, building, and industry. Only if the region in question is unproductive, boggy, too hot, too cold, too steep, or too anything else to be much use for speculation or development, does the conservation movement have a chance.

In countries where land ownership is constantly changing and where small tribes live isolated and sometimes nomadic lives, the conservation movement

faces yet another ethical dilemma. The question is should the home, the central pivot of the way of life of a people, be interfered with to further the aims of wild life or environmental conservation?

Let us look at this problem more closely by again considering the situation in parts of Africa. Before white settlers came to colonize Africa, many tribes had already set aside certain areas as the homes of their chief spirits or gods. These sacred areas were mostly situated in dense forests or caves or on high mountains and no human being was allowed to go there; those who did were punished. The white colonists paid little attention to the holy places of the natives and violated them in the interests of geological surveys, exploration, or big-game safaris. Until quite recently, some of them paid for this with their lives. Then they set certain areas aside and many of the largest game reserves were established while the continent was still under colonial rule. The purpose of these reserves was not necessarily understood by the natives, who continued to live by hunting and trading in elephant ivory and rhino horn, as they had always done.

Such conflict between local traditions and conservation is no less serious a problem in many Christian countries. This is because the Judaeo-Christian teaching emphasizes the superiority of man, and implies that only man has a soul, and that other animals do not; it states that man should "have dominion over the fish of the sea . . . the fowl of the air, and . . . every living thing that moveth upon the earth." Fortunately, in Thailand the government is well

Left: Elephant tusks recovered from a poachers' cache. The game warden's helicopter has, in recent years, put an end of the hunter/poacher's dream of making a good living out of elephants.

All over the world, signs such as this (above) make appeals to the better nature of literate visitors. This one is a particularly quaint example and clear to anyone who reads English or Burmese.

Left: The social centre of the game reserve is the water hole. To this one in Serengeti Park, Tanzania, zebra and wildebeeste come to drink and be sociable.

Near right: Mesa Verde National Park, Colorado. "Cliff Palace," largest of the cliff dwellings built by pre-Columbian Indians, dates from the 13th Century, it is said to have had more than two hundred living-rooms plus ceremonial and storage rooms. Visitors wander over the ruins, then go to the museum (p.134). Far right: Visitors can tour the overhanging, water-smoothed cliffs of Glen Canyon recreational area, Colorado, in boats hired out from the Park's Marina (p.134.)

placed to invoke religion in support of conservation: Buddhism, the national religion, teaches that unnecessary killing or cruelty to any animal is wrong. Thus the nature conservation bill recently laid before the Thai parliament emphasizes the value placed by the Buddhist faith on the protection of life; and in this spirit the government intends to mark the boundaries of their reserves by putting up large notices bearing the words "Dedicated to the Lord Buddha."

Reserves and Tourism Land is set aside not only for the sake of wild life and ecologists. Inherent in the idea of a National Park is that it is a place where people can both enjoy themselves and learn to understand and appreciate the natural environment. The conservation movement is concerned with men as well as wild life and it places a great deal of emphasis on man's need and right to return periodically to his pre-technological habitat. Some National Parks, particularly those of America and Africa, specialize in wide open spaces and scenic grandeur. The United States has National Parks and State Parks as well as a variety of other types of reserves; altogether these were visited in 1967 by the staggeringly large number of 139,676,000 people. Currently, about 145 million man-days are spent in the National Parks each year. The official American attitude to their National Parks is laid down in a statute preventing "occupancy or sale under the laws of the United States . . . and dedicated and set apart as a public park or pleasuring ground for the benefit and enjoyment of the people."

But the advantage of a national pleasuring ground is greatly enhanced if it

can be profitable as well; as we have already mentioned, most areas devoted to conservation cannot exist unless they bring in revenue. The income to the State of California was U.S. $850 million in one year from spending in and around the park (part of this money eventually finds its way into the exchequer through taxation). Most countries cannot operate on such a vast scale: Japan, for example, has a rather special type of National Park that has evolved to suit the country's small size and high population density. Unlike Africa and America it cannot afford to set much uninhabited land aside; instead, the Japanese have a system whereby people live and work in these areas almost as they do in non-conservation areas, but the scenery and wild life are protected by the public's good behaviour. Also, where there is enough wild land they have adopted a system of zoning similar to that described on p. 115. With a combined area of 4,360,000 acres, the Japanese national parks occupy nearly 5 per cent of the total area of Japan, and more than 60 million people visit them annually. National parks can be designated irrespective of who owns the land, and limits on building, deforestation, advertising, and other activities can be laid down by the government.

The Australian National Parks are visited by about one million people a year, though there are no up-to-date figures. They are under government control, and are important but not vital to the economy. But the nature reserves and other conservation areas are only under control of individual states, and the few who are aware of the need to preserve the fauna, flora, and habitats in Australia are far outnumbered by the "if it moves shoot it—if it doesn't—well, shoot it anyway" school of thought. Nature reserves, as op-

posed to National Parks, can at any time be handed over to private interests for commercial development without recourse to higher authority.

In the Soviet Union, reserves are under national control and are mostly not publicized as pleasure grounds; the aim is to keep conservation areas as quiet as possible so that natural conditions are not destroyed.

It is in Africa that both some of the least enlightened attitudes and some of the most practical and hard-headed attitudes to conservation are found. In an underdeveloped and largely tribal country the conflicts and pressures against environment protection are tremendous and many countries cannot yet cope with the economic demands that a conservation programme would make initially. Thus it has been, and still is, most important to convince the heads of state of such countries that National Parks can eventually (after initial outlay) be immensely profitable as a renewable natural resource. Jomo Kenyatta of Kenya says that he is personally interested in wild life and pays frequent visits to the Nairobi Park. He is also well aware of the use, both of wild life as a natural resource and of tourism as a profitable source of income and foreign currency. Julius Nyerere of Tanzania said as long ago as 1960: "I personally am not very interested in animals. I do not want to spend my holidays watching crocodiles. Nevertheless, I am entirely in favour of their survival. I believe that after diamonds and sisal, wild animals will provide Tanzania with its greatest source of income."

The attitude of a National Park administration may be partly to relieve

Left : Mammoth Hot Springs of Yellowstone Park, USA. The water, heated by passing through recently active volcanic rocks, reaches the surface. Lime that was in suspension is discharged grain by grain as Travertine, and gradually these magnificent terraces build up round the spring. Top right : The Ojcow National Park, Poland is famous for its rock formations, such as this one, known as "The Club." Ojcow is one of Polands' lesser known parks

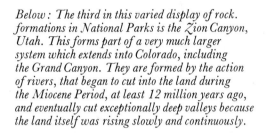

Below : The third in this varied display of rock. formations in National Parks is the Zion Canyon, Utah. This forms part of a very much larger system which extends into Colorado, including the Grand Canyon. They are formed by the action of rivers, that began to cut into the land during the Miocene Period, at least 12 million years ago, and eventually cut exceptionally deep valleys because the land itself was rising slowly and continuously.

tourists of their money, but this is not the only aim. National Parks do provide a valuable service to the public. A well-run park provides not only facilities for having fun but also a chance for tourists to learn something of the natural history of the area. There are usually publicity leaflets available for most National Parks, many showing bathing beauties, camping sites, and speed-boat races as well as photographs of the scenic wonders and other amenities. But very few parks cater for the really interested visitor who would welcome more detailed and specialized information. In response to this real need, information available to visitors should include a detailed map and guide to the park. Where there is a cave or a spectacular rock formation there should also be a general geological map together with an explanation of interesting features and of how the phenomenon came into being, together with details of any localities where fossils can be freely collected. Guides to the flora and fauna of the park should be available for sale or hire. If an archaeological site is excavated and open to visitors, it should have a site map and the levels should be labelled; even to someone familiar with archaeological techniques an unlabelled excavation may well look like a crisscross of meaningless walls and roofless rooms (all movable objects such as bones and pottery are usually removed to a museum to protect them from weather and theft). So reconstructions help the public to see how the original structure might have looked.

Many National Parks cater especially for people interested in the local wild life; it is surprising how many people know almost nothing about the natural history of their own country or even region. Not so long ago a 70-year-old Tanzanian admitted to a well-known conservationist that he had never seen a lion. Apparently 90 per cent of all children in Tanzania never get to know the wild animals of their land and although European children have often seen quite a lot of big-game animals in the zoos, they too have often not seen their own local animals in the wild. There are small parks in South Africa, Britain, Malagasy, Australia, and elsewhere in which typical local species are exhibited in their natural habitat, mainly for schoolchildren.

Man and Beast   National Parks have had a lot of teething troubles regarding the problem of mixing tourists and wild animals. After all many of these parks have been set aside for a number of different purposes; to combine them all successfully is by no means easy.

In the early days of the Kruger National Park, for instance, visitors were allowed a great deal of freedom and allowed to leave their cars and to wander about the park on foot. The animals were, apparently, most tolerant of this invasion upon their preserves. On one occasion, however, a picnic party was photographed sitting among the rocks some little way from the road, and when the film was developed it showed an interested spectator—a lion only about 10 feet away in the bush. From this time on it was decided that visitors should stay in their cars, and the animals soon found that the humans in cars meant no harm and that the cars themselves were not edible. So they stopped being afraid and began to enjoy watching human beings parading

Left: A tourist in the Nairobi National Park, Kenya, photographs a lioness. Right: Tourists with a bear on the road near Lake Louise, Canada. The aim of these parks is to allow visitors to get close to wild animals while maintaining safety precautions.

for them. Visitors to the Kruger and many other game reserves have to keep to the roads and also to obey certain regulations—for instance, a speed limit has been imposed, to prevent the raising of too much dust on the dirt roads. Driving at night may be prohibited, because the animals can be dazzled by headlights so that they become immobilized by the glare and get run over. The interesting flora and fauna of the Kruger and other similar parks bring thousands of visitors each year. They drive slowly along dusty roads peering out into the bush, hoping for a sight of one of the great cats, and becoming ever increasingly blasé about the impala and other buck, wildebeste, bison, and warthogs, as well as the hippos that doze in the murky rivers. Vultures wheeling overhead signify a "kill" and car-loads of onlookers may sit for hours on the roadside hoping for a sight or sound of the food chain in action.

Another great favourite of both African and Asian National Park visitors is the elephant. The Indian elephant is relatively harmless but the African species should be approached (if at all) with extreme caution. In India and Ceylon the paths that the elephants take through the jungle are protected territory; in fact wherever there are elephants, they hold sway. The African elephant can easily become enraged and dangerous to human beings even in cars, which they are quite capable of squashing simply by sitting on them. One part of the Kruger Park (formerly called the Shingwedzi Reserve) is a favourite spot for elephants. Large stretches of this area look as though a hurricane had struck them—elephants love young green shoots of trees and uproot whole trees in order to get them. They also have a decided penchant

for the berries of the marula tree, which, when ripe, are intoxicating; the elephants totter about "high" and uncontrolled. (Warthogs, too, are "hooked" on these berries.) Not long ago, a zoologist colleague dropped the lens cap of his camera in the bush in elephant country close to the reserve; a cow elephant was disturbed when he returned for it and chased him over about 300 yards of rough country. It was gaining on him when he managed to jump into a narrow donga (dry river bed) and the elephant passed clean over his head because it could not stop suddenly.

To open a game reserve to the public does mean a fair amount of interfering with nature, in that roads must be built, and rest centres and camping sites must be enclosed for protection from nocturnal prowlers. The public are usually instructed that they must not feed the animals and they do not make the wardens' job easier by disobeying. It would not seem to be doing much harm, for example, to feed a banana to a baboon—especially when it seems so tame, jumping onto the car and eyeing the occupants with lively curiosity. But it is doing harm because a baboon that relies on bananas during the tourist season will not be as efficient at finding food for itself during the summer, when heat or tsetse fly make the reserve unfit for tourists. Even

Fujiyama, sacred mountain of Japan, is an inactive volcano 12,388 feet high. It stands in a great National Park, and is also a centre for an annual pilgrimage of more than 50,000 people. This view is from the Koma-gatake protected area.

visitors who understand the ecological repercussions that their actions might have, will often be won over by the appealing eyes of a small furry creature. In the United States and Canada there are National Parks where both bears and people roam freely. Rangers labour endlessly to convince the tourists that bears are dangerous. But the public cannot resist feeding, coaxing, and encouraging the bears. There have, over the years, been some severe casualties and a large number of cases of scratching and mauling, usually after definite provocation—but the undaunted public remain enthusiastic.

Camera Safaris Some parks provide a motor or boat service not for hunting but simply for game spotting. These have become known as "camera safaris"; photography is the only type of "shooting" permitted. Transport in Indian National Parks may also be by elephant. One tourist guide book to Indian wildlife sanctuaries gives helpful hints on how to relax and sway when riding on elephant-back so as to go on for hours without getting tired.

Game spotters are accommodated at camps or guesthouses. In some larger game parks there are tree hides where visitors can climb onto a platform and watch game at night, sometimes by flashlight and sometimes only by moon-

Tourists to Kruger National Park, South Africa, put up for the night at camps such as this. In general, meals are eaten outdoors (baboons try to infiltrate the camp to steal food); at night one can lie and listen to the sound of the bushveld.

light. These hides are usually built in a strategic place—next to a water hole, for instance, where animals come to drink, play, and kill each other. In Thailand, experienced game spotters known facetiously as "hunters" can be hired (together with searchlights) to take visitors on a nocturnal safari around the Khao Yai National Park.

But when most people think of National Parks, they do not think of game and game spotting, research or staring at archaeological ruins; they think of wide open spaces, getting away from it all, hiking, camping, and so on. Enjoyment of the outdoors is certainly what brings most of the visitors to the United States National Parks every year. Even in many of the under-developed countries there are huge areas set aside for public enjoyment. Crowds throng to the parks for holidays, weekends, and even day trips, to get away from the cities and from their fellow men. But can one get away from it all—or are there just too many people? In American conservation circles there is a saying: "The Americans love their National Parks so much, they're ruining them!"

Let us look at one of the great National Parks—Yosemite, with its thundering waterfalls and steep wooded mountains. On an average summer weekend, Yosemite is visited by upward of 40,000 people—almost all of whom come by car, blocking the access roads for many miles around. Once in Yosemite valley the problem is to find a parking space somewhere in the concreted acreage of car park. There are hotels, cabins, a hospital, several souvenir stalls, two paved roads, shops, and an outdoor amphitheatre. All these have been added to Yosemite's natural splendours because members of the affluent society are not prepared to rough it, and demand the comforts of home, even in the wilderness. In the evening the valley lies beneath a pall of exhaust fumes and campfire smoke. Tents are pitched end to end; pots and pans clatter to the sound of transistor radios—and even television sets. Only after campers have gone to bed can the roar of the waterfall and the sound of the wind in the trees be heard. In contrast to this there is a certain National Park—Isle Royale, an island of half a million acres in Lake Superior—on which there are no roads. It is visited by only 13,000 people per year.

The great ideal of the American National Park was conceived in an age when places like Yosemite could be penetrated only by two hard days on horseback. Now the ideal is collapsing in the face of the motor car and sheer numbers of people. Although, as we have said, 145 million man-days are spent in American parks each year, the vast majority of visitors try to take in as many national parks as possible in a single trip, spending only a day in each, viewing the scenery through the windscreen, stopping only to take photographs, and keeping to roads and camping sites. These people never wander into real wilderness. Is this the end-product of the great heritage of which Americans are so proud? Are the National Parks in other countries also doomed to become an extension of suburbia? If the increase of human populations threatens the existence even of National Parks—the most carefully controlled environments on earth—what are its effects likely to be elsewhere?

Above: The Marina at Glen Canyon National recreation area. Below: The museum "Spruce Tree House" at Mesa Verde. A diorama model of the cliff dwellings is reconstructed to give a more rounded idea of the way of life of the pre-Columbian Indians.

135

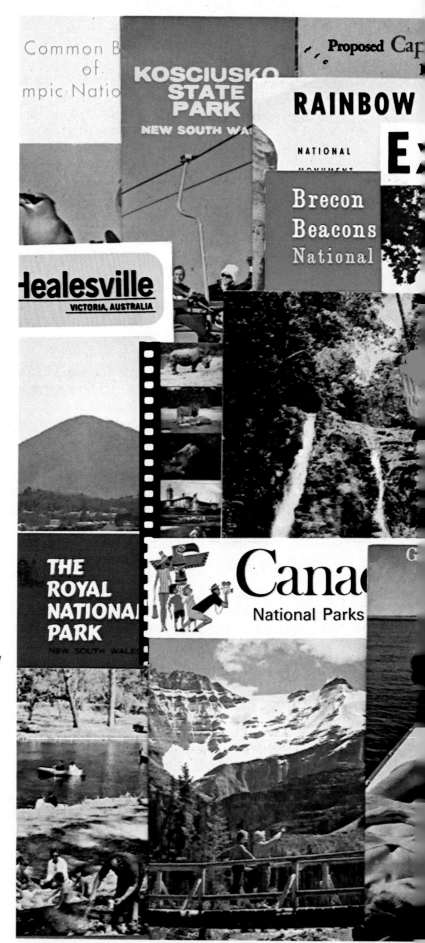

A selection of leaflets, guides and advertizing material for National Parks in various parts of the world. It is conspicuous that some of the parks most famous for their wildlife, tend to advertise, not this, but the sports and recreational facilities. At the top left corner is an illustrated booklet on birds in the Olympic Park, USA.; but the general appearance of the material is the same as that of holiday resort brochures.

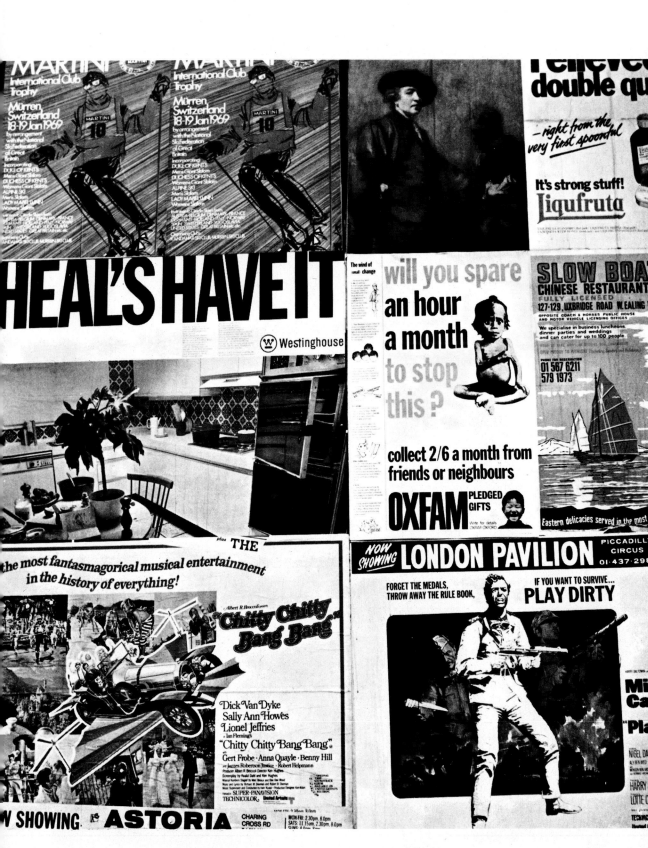

Now we must consider the Conservation of Man; the dilemma caused by the growing avalanche of people. Hunger, poverty, social disintegration, the irreversible destruction of our environment; these are our priorities in the next generations.

138

CHAPTER 7

ONE+ONE=MILLIONS

Today we are constantly bombarded with advertising, stop-press news, and sensation—on posters, in the press, on radio, in the cinema, but especially on television. Every few minutes, it seems, someone demands that we "consume"; triumphs and catastrophes large and small are paraded before our eyes. The result is a surfeit, a maze we can no longer penetrate. It is also one of the strange effects of surfeit that we can watch scenes of unspeakable horror and misery that we know to be happening here and now—and we hardly feel a reaction any more; we remain detached and uninvolved. So when we hear the words *population explosion* or see pictures of starving children, these images are already so familiar that they take their place alongside the countless trivialities that occupy us for a few moments before our attention is directed to something else.

Until a very few years ago we were lulled into believing that man, aided by his technology, could expand and progress indefinitely; the earth, we were told, could contain and feed limitless numbers of people. There are several reasons why experts have changed their minds; but the principal one is that, until quite recently, nobody predicted the rate of population growth in any realistic terms. Meanwhile we have quite outstripped even the most daring prophecies. Also food supplies and other resources are not keeping up with demand; but although the provision of adequate food for the present and future must be looked on as a top priority, it cannot be regarded as the only target; more food means more people to breed and still more to feed and this can lead only to ecological disaster. The need for the population control is imperative. But human society is based on a variety of traditions and values, and the changes that are needed strike at the most deeply ingrained customs of marriage and family structure. These changes must come if the earth is to remain habitable, but the problem is how to achieve them without destroying the values that hold individuals and societies together, and thereby making life meaningless.

Let us first set the scene by considering where people live, and why. The study of populations is called *demography*, and on the next two pages a demographic map of the world shows population distribution and densities.

Population Controls All species are capable of breeding at a rate that could over-populate the earth in a few generations. This is because an unchecked population increases by *geometrical progression*. The simplest example of this progression is to be found in a bacterial culture because bacteria breed by dividing in half. But in natural communities there are many ways in which, by natural selection and other mechanisms, plant and animal populations are regulated. In certain types of community, where the balance between food and population is delicately poised, there is an automatic response to increased numbers and food shortage, and this response operates over and above a reduction in population through starvation. What happens is that certain animals such as lemmings, voles, and rabbits are able to adjust their own rate of breeding in order to meet an emergency. This process is called *internal fertility control*. For a time, when there is plenty of food, the birth-rate is fairly high, but eventually pressure of food and lack of space causes fewer young to be born. How this is achieved is a mystery; overcrowding in rabbits was studied under laboratory conditions and it was discovered that embryos that had already begun to develop were reabsorbed and were never born. Another interesting fact is that, in years when the fertility of these animals is high, the fertility of their predators is also

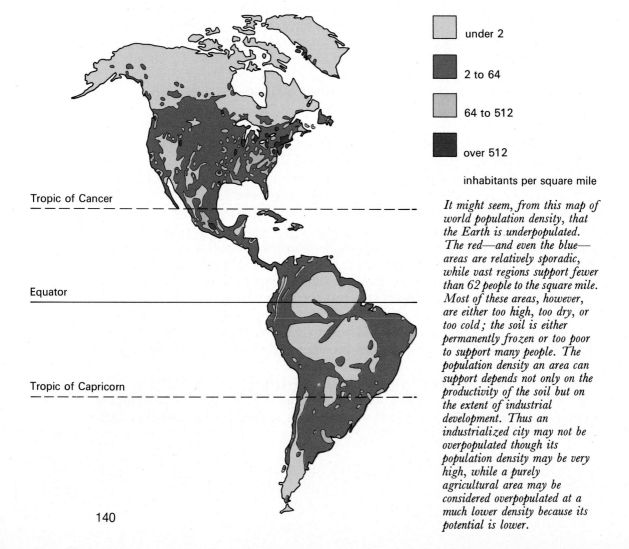

under 2

2 to 64

64 to 512

over 512

inhabitants per square mile

Tropic of Cancer

Equator

Tropic of Capricorn

It might seem, from this map of world population density, that the Earth is underpopulated. The red—and even the blue— areas are relatively sporadic, while vast regions support fewer than 62 people to the square mile. Most of these areas, however, are either too high, too dry, or too cold; the soil is either permanently frozen or too poor to support many people. The population density an area can support depends not only on the productivity of the soil but on the extent of industrial development. Thus an industrialized city may not be overpopulated though its population density may be very high, while a purely agricultural area may be considered overpopulated at a much lower density because its potential is lower.

high. But when natural fertility controls suppress the population growth, the predator temporarily checks its own breeding rate in response: for instance, the snowy owl of Canada fails to lay eggs if there is a shortage of lemmings. This pattern of fluctuating fertility is also known as *cyclicism*. Man, lacking the benefit of internal fertility control, must work out his own solutions. His dilemma is not made easier by the fact that he is not prepared to harden his heart and do to his own kind what he does to other animals that over-populate their habitat: he cannot, or will not as yet, crop his own species. He has to face his crisis without recourse to mass euthanasia, selective nuclear bombing, or any of the other ghoulish "solutions" that have sometimes been suggested.

The present crisis is actually quite recent in origin; in the past, human populations were, to a large extent, kept under control by natural or "Malthusian" checks—named after Thomas Malthus (p. 14). The principal checks have always been famine and disease. Famines occur from time to time because of crop failure, and their efforts are all the more drastic if the human population in the famine area is already excessive. Disease takes two forms, and the more conspicuous is the epidemic: the Black Death, for instance, killed one quarter of the population of Europe in the 14th century,

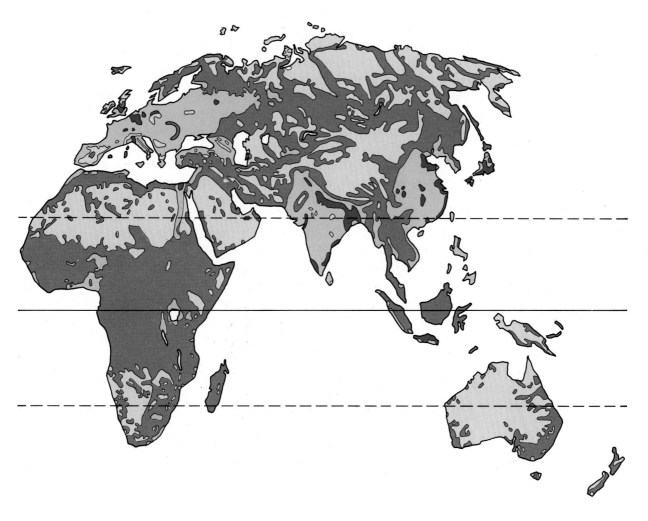

and the cholera epidemic of a hundred years ago killed 45 out of every 1000 Londoners. Wars in themselves have seldom acted as effective checks, but the aftermath of war has often taken the form of massive famines and epidemics, in which many more people have died than were killed in battle. But though the effect of epidemics is more spectacular, the biggest single control of human population has been *endemic* disease, which has taken a steady toll of human lives from infancy on.

It is difficult to realize how effectively these natural checks regulated human populations and how recently the change has come about. It is only in this century that changes in medical science, communications, and technology have increased man's ability to control famine and disease, and the result has been a sharp increase in population, and hence a food shortage in many parts of the world.

Europe's Ups and Downs To understand the background to the present problems we must go back to 17th-century Europe, where a complex series of slow changes, now known as the *demographic transition*, was beginning to take place. Following on the beginning of the Industrial Revolution, the pace of industry began to increase right across Europe and beyond. New continents were opened up, and from them came additional food and raw materials; commerce expanded and with it came improvements in transportation that allowed food and capital goods to be carried longer distances than ever before. Over the next two centuries technology moved into agriculture and industry, and food began to be mass-produced for the first time. Improved housing and sanitation in the mid-19th century gradually led to control of some diseases, and small improvements came also in the medical sciences.

These developments were welcomed wholeheartedly, but they upset the balance that had kept population down during the previous centuries. So, following the drop in the death rate, life expectation went up, infant mortality went down, and the population of Europe rose. However, after about 1875 there was a noticeable reversal of the former upward trend; the population *declined* dramatically and this decline lasted until World War II.

What brought this about? On the superficial level one could say that it was due to the increased production of contraceptives and their increased use by the poorer classes. But this was only the means to an end, so to speak, and the trend had its roots in the deeper social changes that were taking place due to the Industrial Revolution. Why is this relevant to our present population crisis? Because there are some similarities between the social structure of 18th- and 19th-century Europe and that of today's underdeveloped regions. Europe's history does not, however, give us all the answers, because there are also many very basic differences, as we shall shortly see.

Before the Industrial Revolution, Europe consisted of agricultural communities, with here and there a town that had grown up around natural resources such as coal or iron deposits. Most families were tied to the land and they had to have many children because sons were needed to work on the farm and daughters were needed for the dairy and other indoor work. Also, disease took such a heavy toll that large families were necessary for survival; only two children might survive out of, say, ten born; there was no social security and parents relied on their children to keep them in their old age. Thus large family units consisting of several generations all lived and worked together.

But, as industrialization spread through Europe, more and more people left the land for work in the towns. The traditional rural family structure broke up; urban communities developed and these became based on the new and smaller units of parents and children. As the urban children grew up they trained for trades or professions, but did not usually need to stay to help their parents as they did in the farming society. All this meant that there was a general reduction of emphasis on early marriage and continuous child-bearing and there was also an increased burden on the father to support his wife and family (every child had to be fed, clothed, and educated at the father's expense). This was a tremendous factor in reducing the number of children per family. In fact it has been said that materialism is the greatest incentive to planned families. When a family is very poor, and has low expectations from life, the tendency is to have many children. When the income is slightly higher and is coupled with the thirst for capital goods and possessions, the number of children decreases. Only in very wealthy families with the means to gratify greed for material possessions does the family size go up again.

There were, during the whole period, new areas of land to colonize; America became the largest overspill country in the world, receiving a very large number of Europeans. The colonies of Africa and South America also received a fair-sized quota of immigrants from over-crowded Europe and, one way and another, this all helped to prevent a demographic disaster. Even so, Europe remains one of the most densely populated regions on Earth.

Right: The dead being carted off in Palermo, Sicily, during the cholera epidemic of 1835. In this century we have seen such progress in medicine, that many of the once common causes of death have been eradicated over much of the world. We have therefore lost a certain familiarity with death, which we may have to regain, in the next few generations.

While emigration may have solved Europe's problems in the 19th century, it does not solve anything today, because any major movement of peoples is largely blocked by political boundaries and immigration policies. There is still a fair amount of physical space available but the Earth is no longer a single reservoir, open to all.

Because of these barriers, the population problem has become acute in some areas before it has affected other areas at all. If there were no barriers to population redistribution there might be no problem. As it is, there is no single solution that can apply equally to all nations and peoples.

How Many People?   Today there are only a few places on Earth where the birth-rate is stable or decreasing; everywhere else it is increasing to some extent. At present (1968) the population of the world is estimated at over 3500 million. Two babies are born every second; the world population goes up by 5 million a month (1 million of these are in India alone). By the year 2000 there may be between 6500 and 7000 million people on Earth. Several demographers have tried to dramatize the recent increase in world population by estimating the maximum numbers the Earth could hold provided existing resources were fully utilized. These estimates range very widely; one of the lowest, 2800 million (made in 1945), was overtaken about 10 years later. Several others, ranging from 5000 to 7000 million, will almost certainly be exceeded by the end of this century. The largest estimate —50,000 million—once thought to be in the realms of fantasy, will be reached at the present rate of increase in only 150 years. All the estimates except the last were made of the maximum number that could be supported without substantially lowering the standard of living. But it is almost inevitable that before very long the numbers of people in the world will be supported only by a general lowering of standards all round, including those of the affluent nations.

How are these estimates made? Let us look at this in more detail. Demographers usually calculate the fertility index of a population by estimating the *crude birth-rate*—the number of babies born for every thousand of the population in a given period of time, usually one year. This figure gives a rough idea of the increase of population due to births, but it can be very misleading. For instance it takes no account of the sex or age composition of the population and this can make all the difference. A birth-rate of, say, 30 per 1000 only tells you that for every 1000 of the population there is an average increase of 30, making 1030 after one year.

But in rapidly growing populations there is a proportionately large number of children. In any sample of 1000 people, one half will be males, and we can disregard these in calculating the birth-rate. If more than, say, 30 per cent of the female population are less than 15 years old, and 10 per cent are too old to breed, it means that only 300 of the 500 women are of breeding age, so the birth-rate actually reflects an increase of 30 children per 300. Another country may have a far smaller proportion of the population

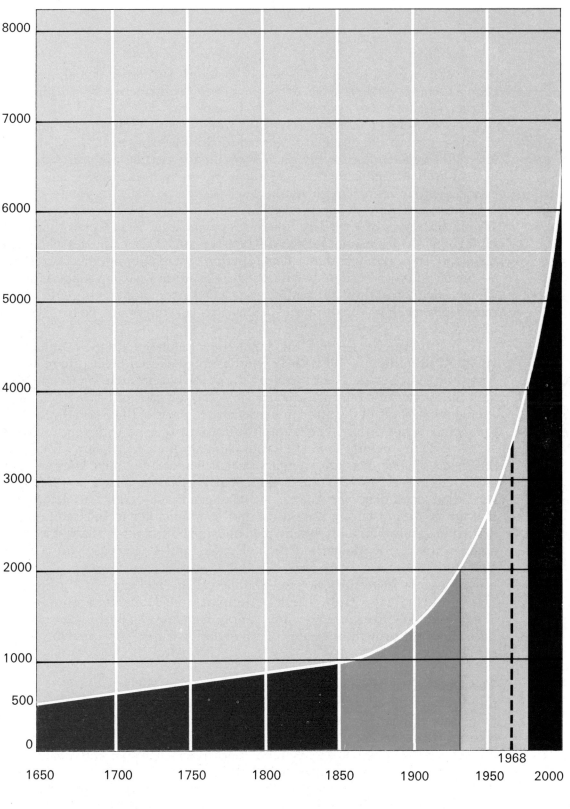

8000							
7000							
6000							
5000							
4000							
3000							
2000							
1000							
500							
0							

1968

1650 1700 1750 1800 1850 1900 1950 2000

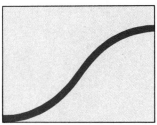

First look (left) at this "normal curve," typical of population distributions where natural controls are in force, and the population—after an initial steep rise—levels off. Now see the "exponential curve" of human population, after natural checks cease to be effective. Note that the doubling time of the population gets shorter each time; numbers will double again before the year 2000.

above and below breeding age—and the number of fertile females will be proportionately higher. Thus the same crude birth-rate figure will, in fact, reflect a smaller percentage of children being born.

A better way of indicating fertility would be to relate the number of children born to the number of women of child-bearing age (15–48) and to ignore the rest. Unfortunately the first method is used because it is easier, so it is as well to understand the method and to recognize its pitfalls when comparing one country with another.

World Patterns of Fertility   Birth-rates vary from 10 to 60 per thousand. Unfortunately one cannot rely on data from many of the countries where the birth-rate is probably highest. This is because people do not always register all births and also because accurate censuses are not easy to make in areas where villages are tiny and remote. Even so, some countries in Africa have recorded very high birth-rates—Guinea 62 per thousand, Niger 61, and Ghana 56.

In South America, where the population increased from 91 million in 1920 to 218 million in 1961, there is an average overall birth-rate of 45: in Asia the average is 41. These birth-rates are clearly very high when compared with the average for Europe, which is 19. Although Europe has a much lower average than some of the more underdeveloped parts of the world, even there the picture is not simple. For example in Eastern Europe both very high and very low birth-rates are found. That of Hungary is extremely low (12·9) and this seems strange, because Hungary is classified as a Catholic country. The main reason for this low rate is that abortion was legalized in 1956. The legislation states that every married woman can make a conscious determination on the size of family she wants, and it permits her to interrupt an undesired pregnancy by means of induced abortion. Similar laws have since been made in the USSR, Bulgaria, Czechoslovakia, and Yugoslavia—all between 1955 and 1960.

The highest birth-rates are in Albania (41·2), Iceland (25·8), Portugal (24·7), and Ireland (21·8). The lowest, apart from Hungary, are in Sweden (14·2) and West Berlin (11·1). But simply knowing the birth-rate tells you little about the growth or decline of a population unless you know the death-rate as well.

The Decline in Mortality   The phenomenon we know as death-control is the direct result of recent medical progress, and, because it is universally more acceptable than birth-control, it has far more effect on population changes than declines or fluctuations in the birth-rate. The decline in mortality affects people of all ages; more babies survive and people live longer and breed for a longer period. It is thus the drop in the death-rate that is almost entirely responsible for the present "explosion"; the birth-rate itself has remained almost unchanged. Although the *crude death-rate* is—as with the birth-rate—calculated per thousand of the population, it is, if anything,

146

more difficult to measure, partly because it is difficult to distinguish between still-births (and late foetal deaths) and deaths of persons born alive. Also there is a tendency for people (especially in remote areas) not to register all deaths. The United Nations estimates that only about 33 per cent of the world's deaths and 42 per cent of births are ever registered.

There is an increasing tendency for the drop in mortality to level out, in the more developed countries at any rate. Declines that began first in Europe (excepting Russia) have certainly levelled out there in the present century. In other parts of the world, however, death-control has only begun in the last two decades and, because of the youthful age structure, the declines have been spectacular.

Mortality has not declined everywhere equally, and unfortunately in those countries where it has done so most dramatically there has all too often been no corresponding rise in the standard of living. It also tends to be higher in rural areas than in towns, because most doctors and hospitals are based on centres of population.

There are two main causes of death; one is environmental, the other degenerative. The environmental deaths occur mostly in underdeveloped countries where infectious diseases are still rampant, living conditions are poor, and food shortages occur. Degenerative deaths—such as heart disease, cancer, and sheer old age—on the other hand, occur mostly in countries in which death-control is well advanced. In fact people who die of these ailments usually do so because they have not died of anything else first.

Death-control has been heralded as an unequalled triumph of medical science over nature, but it is no longer looked upon with such naive optimism as it once was. It is now seen to be a two-edged sword, as many people are beginning to realize, and it cannot be welcomed wholeheartedly *unless it is matched by birth-control.*

As the population map shows, the areas coloured red are those where the population is most dense and where the problem is generally most urgent. Much of Europe, however, despite its high population density, is no longer in a state of emergency. What can Europe's ups and downs teach the rest of the world? In fact, Europe is the foundation on which all of today's programmes are based. But in certain ways its value as an example is limited. First, its area is comparatively small. Second, the population increased from 120 million in 1650 to only 576 million by 1950; Europe was never dealing in the sort of numbers that Asia is dealing with today. The population of Asia in 1950 was 1389 million and by A.D. 2000 it will probably be about 4250 million as compared with Europe's 987 million. Third, we must remember that changes came slowly in Europe, over more than 200 years of slow industrialization, slow improvement of communications, steady emigration, and increasing awareness of the advantages of reducing population size. But the problem that faces the underdeveloped countries today cannot possibly be solved in the same leisurely way. Fourth, Asia may have an enormous area in contrast to compact Europe, but Asia is already over-crowded and has nowhere to spill to. Finally, the resources of many of the most over-populated areas are played out, partly plundered by Europeans during the colonial period, partly mismanaged through ignorance, and partly exhausted through constant use.

The Cult of Fertility   It is difficult for most of us, who take for granted the influence of western culture and tradition, to visualize the ways of life of communities that are quite different from ours. We are very possibly in danger of underestimating the extent to which traditions and religions provide a framework that holds non-industrialized societies together. In fact they play a much stronger part in the way of life of agricultural and rural people than they do in urban societies. Although almost everywhere western

	1940		1950		1960	
Mexico	44·3	*23·2*	45·5	*16·2*	45·0	*11·4*
Costa Rica	44·6	*17·3*	45·9	*12·2*	42·9	*8·6*
Chile	33·4	*21·6*	34·0	*15·0*	35·4	*11·9*
Venezuela	36·0	*16·6*	42·6	*10·9*	49·6	*8·0*
Ceylon	35·8	*20·6*	39·7	*12·4*	37·0	*9·1*
Malaya	40·7	*20·1*	42·3	*15·9*	37·7	*9·5*
Singapore	45·0	*20·9*	45·4	*12·0*	38·7	*6·3*
Japan	29·4	*16·8*	28·2	*10·9*	17·2	*7·6*

The above table shows changes in birth-rates (left-hand column) and death-rates (right-hand column) over two decades in selected developing countries. Except for Japan, the birth-rate has tended to rise but only a little, while the death-rates have fallen staggeringly, as a result of medical progress. It is death control, not any slight rise in birth-rates that has caused the population avalanche. Right: The process shown diagrammatically, (birth-rate purple, death-rate red).

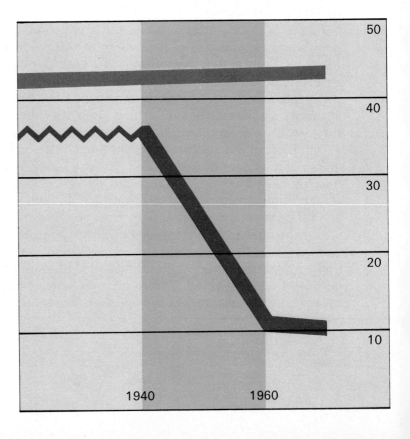

influence is encroaching and bringing change on many fronts, really basic changes are not so easily made, for the traditional roots go deep.

As we already know, the need for many children in rural societies has always been a matter of survival. Not only is a plentiful supply of children needed for a labour force, but there is also a demand for sons as warriors in societies where manpower means military strength. The survival element becomes inextricably bound with tradition and religion. Children become a status symbol: mothers of large families are fêted, and the father is honoured for his virility, and his status in the community increases.

In societies where there are established structures of marriage and paternity, great emphasis is often put on procreation; indeed many religions, among them Catholicism, look on procreation as being the basic reason for

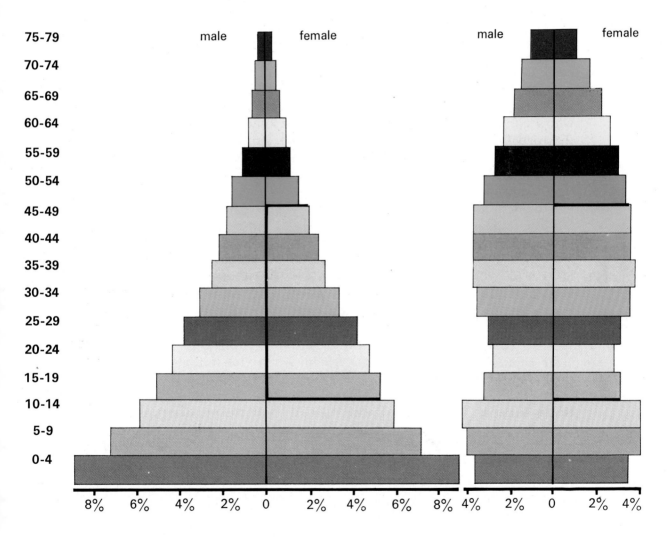

Pyramid diagrams show features of population at a glance. Left: Costa Rica in 1955 shows the high birth-rate (broad base), the high death-rate (tapering apex) and general increase in population, (widening towards base). Right: Sweden in 1956; lower birth-rate (narrow base), high life-expectancy (broader apex), postwar "bulge" (broadening at age groups 10–14 and 5–9). Thick lines demarcate child-bearing age.

marriage. Some allow one man to have only one wife; others, such as Islam and Hinduism, permit several—a type of marriage known as *polygyny*, which is practised in many of the most densely populated parts of the world, and which encourages a high birth-rate.

Just how embedded the idea of fertility is in the social and religious life of India can be judged by a traditional greeting to a Brahmin girl—"be the mother of eight sons and may your husband live long." The other side of the coin, the shame and suffering of the childless, is dramatically shown by the South African writer Ronald Segal in his book *The Crisis of India* (1965): "The plight of the childless woman is only less pitiful than the spinster or, even worse, the widow, and there can be few sights in India as moving as that of a tree bearing the offerings of the barren like a crop of prayers. The childless endure any humiliation or trial in pursuit of divine intervention. In one south Indian ceremony, held every year, the barren women, bathed by their families in the village tank, lie face downwards on the main village road, their arms extended above their heads, their hands together and holding plantains, coco-nut, and betel leaves. At last the priest, accompanied by shouting and drumming, and bearing a tall phallic symbol and covered with marigolds on his head, walks along the road stepping on the backs of the prostrate women, who are then lifted up by their husbands and sometimes carried further down the road for a second "step." On the other hand, the pregnant women is regarded as auspicious and receives respect in public, while the woman who has produced a child, especially a son, acquires a new value both within the family and in Hindu society at large."

Although, in India and elsewhere, death-control has caused a phenomenal fall in infant mortality, somehow this fall has not been comprehended fully. It takes longer than one would think for a population to realize that far fewer of its children are dying. Furthermore even if this fact is grasped it still takes a very big effort to throw off the traditions that go with the cult of the large family. Fertility rites, phallic symbols, and the rest have always been part of the way of life, and art and architecture are not easily eradicated— certainly not without the loss of a good deal besides unwanted children. In such a setting what chance has birth-control? Can its importance be made clear enough to people so that it becomes more meaningful to them than their traditions and religion?

Birth-control   In spite of all we have said about the importance of fertility, we must add that birth-control is by no means unknown in preliterate societies (societies that have no written language). Unfortunately methods have never been really effective, but they have sometimes been inventive; they range from a variety of herbs that induce abortion or reduce fertility, to a favourite Chinese method as follows: "Fresh tadpoles hatching in the spring should be washed with pure well water and then swallowed whole three or four days after menstruation. If a woman swallows fourteen live tadpoles on the first day and ten more on the next, she will not conceive for

Above: the Venus of Laussel, Dordogne (left) shows how ancient is the cult of fertility. She holds a horn in her hand—a very common phallic or male fertility symbol. Today the cult continues; Chief Khotsa of South Africa, pictured with his wives.

Bottom picture: In European agricultural societies today, the large families are still needed to work on the land. This crowd of Sicilian farmers all live together in a small farmhouse. There are about twenty in all including the children.

five years. If the dosage is repeated the following month she will be forever sterile. "This method," the manual says, "is safe, effective and cheap; its only defect is that it can be used only in the spring."

The Chinese began using this method when their other chief means of population control, infanticide—by exposing girl babies at birth—was stopped. This practice—which, incidentally, is quite painless—is probably still going on in Tibet and possibly in other parts of the world as well. In the west, too, infanticide was quite common—more common, perhaps, than is realized. Babies with physical deformities were almost invariably exposed (remember Oedipus); this was an extremely efficient alternative to natural selection, which does not operate in humans nearly so efficiently as in other animals and in plants. But, resourceful though people have been, they have

Top: Posters like this one from Turkey are a vital part of any Family Planning Campaign.
Below left: A mobile clinic in Kuala Lumpur, where women can get advice on family planning and be fitted with contraceptives.

not conquered the problem that now faces us. A world programme is needed; there are still far too many countries not reached by any family planning activities whatever.

As far as possible, it is better to plan a birth-control programme with the support of the government and religious authorities. Of the most influential religions in the world today—Islam, Hinduism, Confucianism, Judaism, Buddhism, and Christianity—only a few sects have any doctrinal objection to artificial methods of birth-control. Of these sects, only the Roman Catholic Church has much real influence, and the 1968 papal encyclical *Humanae Vitae* has remained obdurately opposed to any change in the law. In Catholic countries, family planning activities must and do continue without the church's sanction. Elsewhere, traditions still present a tremendous barrier,

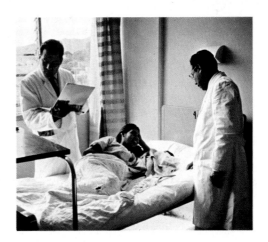

Left: A group of women at an instruction class on contraceptive techniques given by a midwife at a clinic in Chile. Top: A social worker on a home visit to a family living in one of Chile's most overcrowded urban areas. Below right: A ward in a new Mexican hospital, which specializes in family planning and maternal welfare.

but family planning programmes can at least be launched and carried out under government auspices.

The general attitudes of society to women as chattels and child-bearers must be changed first, and this means aiming propaganda at men as well as women. But the fight against rising population is not solely a fight to overcome religious and traditional objections to birth-control. It is a fight to improve general education levels and living standards of the majority of the world's people. For at the very roots of the population problem is the feeling of helplessness and despondency that prevails among the poor, hungry, overcrowded, and wretched of the earth. Any programme of population control must take this into account, and indeed it must begin by encouraging people to find a reason for making a change. It is no easy matter to instill a sense of purpose into people who have lived with their misery for so long. Fatalism is built into many religions, especially those of the east, and the here-and-now must be made to matter, though it undermines reliance on the world to come.

Japan's Success Story   In Asia one country has succeeded in substantially lowering its birth-rate—Japan. Small and over-crowded, Japan made a bid in 1941 to extend its frontiers and failed. The problem was still there, and indeed the returning armies made it worse than ever. By 1948 the population had jumped by 8 million in 3 years, while the birth-rate was 35·5, far higher than that of any other industrial country. Japan seemed to be heading again for disaster, but instead a most remarkable thing happened. In 16 years the birth-rate was reduced to 17·0, a figure lower than that of either Europe or America.

This very considerable achievement was brought about, at first without government support, by the Japanese Family Planning Association, which mounted an efficient propaganda campaign to reduce fertility. Articles appeared in newspapers and women's magazines; talks were given on the radio. There were, of course, occasional outbreaks of counter-propaganda, in which birth-control was objected to for religious or ideological reasons; but the proponents of birth-control were more than a match for the objectors.

To begin with, the reduction in births was largely brought about by illegal abortion, though this was largely replaced by chemical contraceptives, which became available in 1949. In 1951, however, the government became really concerned with the continuing high rate of abortion and its effects on the mother's health, and began to sponsor the family planning programme officially, but with more emphasis on contraception. The budget for family planning in Japan increased from U.S. $ 59,000 in 1952 to U.S. $ 184,000 in 1965. This big programme called for medical and what is known as paramedical staff (such as nurses and midwives). The latter had to be trained, and the midwives especially had to be helped to overcome the feeling that their primary function was that of assisting at births.

The most conspicuous results have been since the war, but the preliminary work was done as early as the 1920s: Japan's high standard of literacy has been a major factor for success, and so has the high level of urban development and industrialization. Japan's example is of only limited use when applied to vast regions such as India, but it was the basis for another campaign that we describe in some detail because it gives some insight into the techniques used in fertility surveys, and also into the small returns for great expenditure of effort.

Trial Campaign   In another small over-populated Asian island, Taiwan, a survey was carried out in 1962–3 to discover people's attitudes to regulating their own families, as a preliminary to a family planning programme. Taiwan has certain similarities with Japan; it is relatively urbanized and industrialized, and literacy and general education levels are quite high. Also Taiwan, like Japan, has good communications and transport and a solid network of medical facilities.

The survey showed that most women had borne more children than they wanted, and that they realized that infant mortality had declined in their communities. People wanted to reduce their family size; all they needed to know was how to do it. A pilot experiment was carried out in the city of Taichung to determine how feasible and costly a nationwide programme would be. First the whole city was exposed to a general distribution of posters and leaflets on the advantages of family planning. Next, research teams (consisting of local health officers and a co-operating team from the United States) divided the city up into over 2000 segments called *lins*. Some were called *nothing lins*—and in these, nothing further was done after the original distribution of posters and leaflets. There were also *mail lins*, in which a direct mail campaign was directed to newly-weds and also to parents with two or more children. In the last category, the *everything lins*, a major effort was made to promote family planning.

Every married woman from 20–39 years old was visited by an especially trained nurse and fieldworker who made an appointment for her to visit a health station provided with a wide variety of contraceptives. The health station also answered any questions and gave advice about family planning. In one half of these everything lins visits were made to wives only. In the other half, both husbands and wives were seen separately or together. The research teams did not encounter very much religious opposition, and, though it was then too early to judge long-term effects, the number of pregnant women went down from 14·2 per cent at the end of 1962 to 11·4 per cent at the end of 1963—a decline of about one fifth. By this time home visits had ceased, but the team kept up a follow-up programme of meetings, and contraceptives remained available at the health centres.

The question is, how well did the campaign succeed? Indeed how would one measure success? At the outset, good intentions could be measured only by the number of people who took advice, bought contraceptives, and expressed their intention of practising contraception. Out of nearly 12,000 homes visited, a total of 5297 women accepted some form of planning.

Over 4000 of them were from within the city of Taichung itself, the rest came from outside; this showed that news of the programme had travelled effectively by word of mouth. But why did so few women from the homes visited take up voluntary birth control as a result of the programme? About 16 per cent were sterile or had been sterilized; 9 per cent were pregnant, and 3 per cent were breast-feeding. Some women actively wanted another child—young wives, or those who had not yet had a son. So in one way or another the final figure for new users of contraception was only about one tenth of the women visited.

The team maintained that if one quarter of the sample can be induced to practice family planning after such a programme, then it has been a great success. They pointed out that the impact of such a programme is not felt immediately; but after an initial period, when word-of-mouth campaigns are well established, the acceptance rate goes up. But even so it stays at a peak for only a short period (in Taichung it was for about four weeks). By then those who are really interested have taken action and the rate declines again (possibly due in part to a surfeit of propaganda).

The Taiwan programme shows cause for both optimism and pessimism. On the credit side, people did not in principle oppose the programme, and 10 per cent of the people visited did respond; should one say "only 10 per cent" or "as much as 10 per cent"? On the debit side, Taiwan, like Japan, is small and compact; the city of Taichung is hardly typical of the vast and squalid rural areas where communications and medical facilities are practically non-existent.

Perhaps the lessons most worth drawing from the experience of Japan and Taiwan as well as that of Europe, are that a campaign to reduce the birthrate must coincide with a general betterment of living standards and education, and that the motivation must come from within each country and not from outside.

This is not to say that help from outside organizations such as the International Family Planning Federation is not essential, but the main task of putting across the ideas and involving the whole populace can be done only by people who understand local ways and customs. These people should, if at all possible, be nationals; outsiders may be regarded with suspicion if they try to introduce a family planning programme. Look, for example, at India, during the time of the British Raj; attempts at regulating population were regarded as a plot to increase the ratio of whites to Indians. To take another instance, if Israel were to implement a birth-control plan throughout her present territory she would be accused of trying to increase the proportion of Jews to Arabs for strategic reasons, because the Arabs breed faster.

Family Planning in India Even a programme that is organized from within takes time to show results, and no-one must expect changes to come overnight. India, in her 15-year plan (1961–76) to reduce her birthrate has put forward a three-point plan. The general aim is to reduce the birth-rate to

Above: When a birth-control campaign initiated from outside is conducted in a country long acquainted with colonialism, there may be reactions like this one at Kingston, Jamaica in 1956.

Right: Use of contraceptives and family size are broadly related to educational level. On this chart the dark green bars represent the number of children women said they wanted; light green bars show the number they had. Red bars show the percentage of each group practising contraception. The figures are taken from the Taiwan survey carried out between 1962 and 1963.

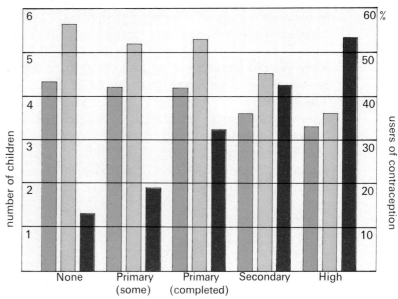

number of children

None   Primary (some)   Primary (completed)   Secondary   High

users of contraception

25 as soon as possible and the general approaches to this goal are as follows: (1) popularizing the various existing methods of contraception and any new ones that might be acceptable in India for mass application; (2) stimulating social changes that have a direct bearing on fertility, such as raising the marriage age of women, improving the status of women and the general level of education, increasing security in old age, and eliminating child labour; (3) accelerating basic economic changes in order to increase per capita income.

This growing awareness of the imperative need for general social and economic development as a companion to any birth-control programme is more than offset in most of the crisis areas by a bottleneck—the lack of doctors and trained personnel. As long as education into methods of birth-control, and the actual fitting or doling out of contraceptives, requires a doctor to see each patient, then not enough people can be reached in time.

The teething troubles of Taiwan have shown how important it is to train even non-medical people in family planning and health organization. In India every effort is being made to train one male and one female "family planning leader" for each village or group of 1000 of the population. The aim is to teach the people to help themselves, and to this end additional "education leaders" have been co-opted to help mobilize public opinion.

Pamphlets, posters, film strips, and exhibitions are used, and these, by all accounts, leave no-one in any doubt as to what is needed to prevent conception and how it can be done. At first, due to almost complete lack of organization, the focus was on birth-control by the safe period method. Subsequently mechanical and chemical contraceptives were brought into use, followed finally by voluntary sterilization, as soon as there were enough doctors to be able to cope.

Even so, progress has so far been very small; India is still only scratching at the surface of the problem. There is some significant improvement in certain towns, notably in Bombay; but Calcutta is a nightmare city where three quarters of the population live in huts or on the streets without tap water or sanitation. Outside the cities, 80 per cent of the population live in remote rural areas and many of these have not yet been reached. On the credit side, the programme is organized by the government, which also gives its full support to the independent Family Planning Association. The will to conquer the problem is there; there is a certain amount of optimism, but whether it is justified or not, time alone will show.

New World Problems Latin America is another danger spot, with many problems quite different from those of India, and many that are similar. The general educational level in much of Latin America is very low and there is as yet not much motivation to reduce the size of families. Unlike India, however, no government is directly sponsoring family planning programmes, and the responsibility for this is left, in general, to the doctors, who are extremely scarce. In several countries there are still legal restrictions on the sale and distribution of contraceptive devices; the Catholic Church favours only "natural methods" of family planning, such as the rhythm method.

Only in Chile (with a birth-rate of 32·8 and death-rate of 11·2) and Colombia (38·0 to 10·0) are well co-ordinated family planning services attempting to cover the whole country. In Chile there is an extremely high illegal abortion rate—reported to be half the birth-rate; it has quadrupled in 30 years. But there is a great deal of research being carried out on the problem of abortion, and it is possible that Chile will make strides in controlling and coming to terms with it—something that Japan did not wholly succeed in doing.

Colombia has mobilized a large-scale training programme for over 1200 doctors and 800 para-medical personnel. As in Japan, public opinion has been stimulated through the mass media and is very receptive to new ideas on contraception. In several other countries, family planning associations exist, and so do private contraceptive services, but so far they are reaching only the urban communities. The problems that are specific to South America are concerned partly with the power of the Catholic Church, and partly with the physical nature of the continent. Almost everywhere in South America, except the relatively literate republics of Argentina and Uruguay, population is accelerating alarmingly, but, unlike India and even Japan, the actual density of population is as yet very low, and the untapped resources of the continent are enormous. Distribution of population is uneven, and growth is much more rapid in the urban areas. The "bands of misery" round many Latin American cities grow thicker, as people leave the rural areas as a result of economic pressures. Improvements in housing, schools, and so on, are absorbed by the rising population as fast as they are completed and in all spheres economic growth is impaired. But this does not mean that Latin America is over-populated—at least, not in the sense that population density is too high, or that there is a lack of resources. A controlled and slower rate of population growth would result in a universal improvement in education and living conditions; many South American countries are potentially extremely productive, and could become major exporters. But today they are still dismally far from this goal.

Emergent Africa The population today is about 330 million. It has risen very steeply since the 19th century, when missionaries infiltrated the continent, bringing medicine and some death-control, but preaching vehemently against any kind of birth-control or abortion. The population has thus boomed wherever their influence was felt, and demographers expect an even sharper rise before any major decline can be expected. This is because the death-rate in parts of Africa is still quite high—in Niger it can be as high as 30, and in the Ivory Coast it is over 33. These countries have birth-rate figures of over 50, so it is easy to see what will happen when medical services improve. As it is, population growth is preventing economic progress in many parts of the continent. Over much of Africa there are no organized family planning associations, either private or government sponsored; in many cases this is due to laws left over from French colonial days. In fact, almost the only countries with family planning facilities are those that have been influenced by Britain, except for the United Arab Republic and Tunisia. In Tunisia family allowances are *stopped* after the fourth child; this is supposed to act as a deterrent to parents who would otherwise have large families.

One of the main barriers to progress is that the remoteness of many communities makes it very difficult for medical services to reach them and there is therefore widespread ignorance of the advantages of family planning and maternal welfare. Where there are centres, they are usually in towns, attached to hospitals, such as the clinics set up in 1967 in Algiers. South of the Sahara, the first independent African government to adopt a national family planning programme was Kenya. They began with a training scheme in 1967 and the clinic programme began in 1968 at the Kenyatta Memorial Hospital, Nairobi. If Kenya's population, now about 9½ million, continues to grow at the present rate (birth-rate 50, death-rate 20), it will double in 23 years; nearly half the entire population is under 15, and this points to an explosion if action is not taken immediately.

The United Arab Republic has a particularly difficult problem with its over-all population at about 30 million. The average birth-rate is over 40, and

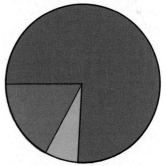

Top: Out of the total population of India in 1961, over 75 per cent were illiterate (purple); of those that received education about 18 per cent were men (red) and 7 per cent women (green). Left: No birth control programme can succeed unless educational standards— especially of women—are improved. Until the role of woman as child-bearer is partly subordinated to her role as a responsible citizen, her only outlet will continue to be as a breeder of large families. But will population increase swamp for ever the chances that the privilege of the few will ever be extended to the many? Right: A Favela or shantytown, clinging precariously to a hillside in a suburb of Rio de Janeiro, Brazil. Is this typical? See Chapter 8.

the death-rate 14·8, and although there is a massive family planning programme under way, the balance is heavily weighted against major improvements in the short term. The general standards of living and education are very low indeed and the impetus to reduce family size is still largely absent among the peasant farming communities that make up the bulk of the population.

Egypt in particular has created an immense problem in the effort to in-increase food production. The Aswan High Dam has been built to extend irrigation, by storing the flood water of the Nile for gradual release during the dry season. But this same dam intercepts the silt plus organic matter that for thousands of years has kept the Nile Valley fertile. The result is that, though there is a gain in water, there is a loss of soil fertility, which will have to be made good by manufacturing artificial fertilizers, using much of the electricity generated at the dam. Such fertilizers are no substitute for the organic matter now trapped with the silt behind the dam; and, to make matters worse, in a few decades the dam will silt up, as dams alway do (there are 2000 silted dams in the United States alone), so that it will no longer even do the job for which it was intended.

Over much of the rest of independent Africa, the International Family

Planning Federation maintains that national governments are hesitant about taking a positive stand, but if private ventures were to get under way and persuade the population (and some of the members of the governments) that it is economically and socially desirable to limit families, then they might in time be amenable to some concerted action. Unfortunately there is no time; the economic expansion desired by these governments will fall further and further behind.

Enigma of China   A major uncertainty is the population of the People's Republic of China. A census carried out in 1953–4 showed a total of 582 million. But this census is widely thought to be inaccurate and incomplete. *If* the birth-rate remained unchanged at 41·6, and *if* the death-rate (20·4 in 1954) declined in the same way as in the rest of Asia, then the population *could* have gone up to 733 million by 1963. If the trend were to continue, the population of China *could* be over 1000 million by 1978, compared with India's 600 million and Brazil's 98 million.

But the "ifs" with reference to the population of China are many. The birth-rate and death-rate may well have been either higher or lower than the figures published in the census. Whatever the birth-rate was, there is no reason to think that it has decreased much since then. The Chinese government's legislation by which couples are not allowed to marry until their late 20s has not been in force long enough to make any substantial difference. The death-rate may have been influenced during the "Great Leap Forward"—but then again, it may not.

One of the problems with China, as with other socialist countries, has been that Marxism-Leninism does not recognize the existence of a population problem. Marx interpreted Malthus's "over-population" as a relative surplus of labour—an essential characteristic of capitalism that would be redressed by correct deployment of manpower and planned use of resources.

Marxists, in theory at least, see the reduction of the birth-rate not as the prime necessity, but as one of many alternative solutions to the problem of mass poverty. Other solutions are to increase economic productivity and to improve health and education. These theories are in direct opposition to Malthus's ideas, on which much of western population theory is based. In many other socialist countries, however, the state accepts the reality of the population problem, and some of them have extremely enlightened family planning services and policies, as we have seen.

To sum up, Malthus's theories are partly out of date now because he could not take into account the tremendous changes that were to occur because of advances in medicine and technology. But no more can we take for granted that these advances will continue to provide for us indefinitely. In the next chapter we shall take a look at some of the things that *are* being done to create an environment fit for us to live in, both now and in the future. But nothing the food scientists, sociologists, or anyone else can do or say will prevent a major disaster unless we limit the growth of the Earth's population.

Today the world is becoming more and more interdependent; if poverty and over-crowding, hunger and deprivation, do not affect you now, it may not be very long before they do. They are already affecting more than two thirds of all people alive (or half alive) today. Statistics tell us, rather comically, that "two and a bit" children per couple is enough to ensure the continuance of the human race. Two would be sufficient to replace each parent; the extra "bit" would take care of any incidental deaths by illness or accident. But people tend to say that statistics are only a lot of numbers that do not affect *them*, that no statistics are going to stop them having a large family if they want to, and anyway everybody should have the freedom to choose for themselves how many children they should have. Well, this word *freedom* is often misused; there are many forms of it, some more basic than others. Those of us who believe in the ideas of conservation say that the freedom to breed as many children as you want, and never mind the generations to come, is lower on the list than freedom from hunger, and freedom to work and to live in decent conditions.

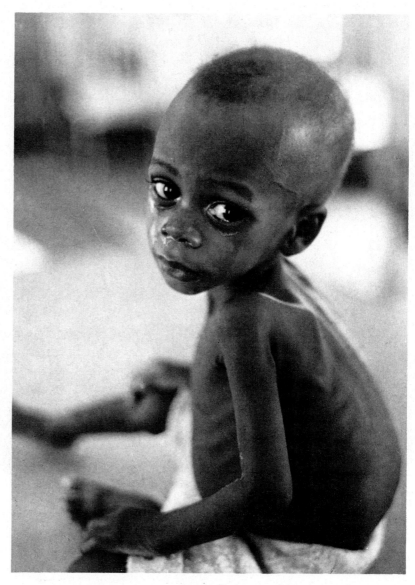

This child is one of the thousands of victims of the war between Nigeria and Biafra. He is also one of the many millions of people who will never have enough to eat, people who are not victims of war, but of their own lack of opportunity or ability to control the size of their families. Out of the population crisis, arise many problems. Some—hunger for example—are not new to us. But others face us for the first time.

Food shortage is, ecologically, a natural result of the population explosion. Our attempts to solve the food problem can only aggravate the problem of overcrowding; more people survive to breed. Are slums to be the environment of the future?

CHAPTER 8

CONSERVATION'S JIGSAW PUZZLE

This chapter is about the survival of mankind in a fast-changing environment. We are concerned here not so much with long-term dreams as with the urgent problems facing us now and in the next few decades. As most of them arise from the increase in world population, it must be remembered that, whatever other remedies may be suggested, these are extras to the all-important need to control the numbers of our own species.

There are no instant solutions in conservation; it is already too late to prevent an ecological crash in India—and perhaps elsewhere too—before this century is over. Indeed one suspects that people will not learn from this tragedy but will simply redouble their efforts to produce large families as an insurance, exactly as in the days before death control.

The majority of conservationists feel that while this crisis is with us, it is conservation's priority to ensure our survival; other aspects, such as protection of wildlife, must inevitably remain the preoccupation of a few dedicated souls. But we cannot afford to ignore any one aspect entirely, because conservation is like juggling; the performer must keep all the clubs in the air. Let one fall and the act is spoilt. The time may yet come when our own survival is assured; then, in retrospect, we shall appreciate the beauty passed down to us through the efforts of wildlife and nature conservationists, even though today we may question their order of priorities.

So far we have tried to show conservation problems from many sides and we have never minimized the difficulties, except perhaps in one particular. We have possibly been too optimistic about the *scale* on which remedies can be applied. On this increasingly crowded planet we can no longer make a clean sweep and start afresh. So conservation practice as we shall see it in this chapter may seem to be piecemeal and disconnected, and fall short of the obvious ideal. But if putting policy into effect means waiting until there are no obstacles in the way (and in the meantime doing nothing) then the Earth may well become uninhabitable in a very few years.

"Hell is Other People"   Each year people leave the countryside and swarm to the cities, or at least into the belts of shantytowns encircling many cities. By 1985 more than half the entire world population will be urban if this trend continues. In these shantytowns the population is growing faster than proper housing and other amenities can be provided. Lima in Peru is only one example of such a city, where a million people have settled in shacks that they have built around the edge of the city's rubbish dump. The horrors of shantytowns are not limited to the underdeveloped countries; in many North American cities there are slums of unspeakable squalor. Already, too, there is a continuous sprawling cancer of mingled city and suburb that is turning into a megalopolis spreading for over 400 miles from Boston to Washington.

Some sociologists say that we shall "adapt" to overcrowding just as we have "adapted" to the increased noise, polluted air, and treeless streets of our cities. Others say that there is a breaking point; the strain of living in cities is becoming intolerable and showing itself in increasing violence. Lord Ritchie Calder said at a recent meeting of the British Conservation Society that by the end of this century town planners would be planning for cities of 1000 million inhabitants and more. Under "ideal" conditions of perfectly planned living accommodation, and scientifically regulated water and air supply and sewage disposal, these cities might be efficient and economical to run. But they would be like the factory farms—"just hutches for battery-fed people," and under such conditions many people would go mad. Which is preferable? Shantytown, megalopolis, or Ritchie Calder's nightmare city? Is there an alternative? It would be fine if cities could be planned from scratch, for reasonable numbers of people, with fresh air and space and amenities. Perhaps a few such new cities will be built, but not many.

No, the main problem facing urban planners is how to improve the environment for city dwellers *within the present cities*; to improve housing and sanitation where possible; to try to widen roads and improve transport; to provide convenient schools and shopping facilities, and to leave green spaces here and playgrounds there.

But, like everyone else, their scope is limited because they are working to a budget, and open space means less housing and loss of income for the landowner. Planners are thus often forced into providing new potential slums to replace the old, almost as cramped and, in today's polluted atmosphere, soon to be just as filthy. Most of the millions living in shantytowns will not even be provided with running water and proper drains—let alone be rehoused—because funds are not available. In the long term, we may yet find that overcrowding is the biggest single problem we have to deal with. Everyone is directly involved and everyone with a conscience can help simply by having no more than two children. It is an absolute must that parents of large families should become the object of social disapproval.

Potential slums. This block of flats in Kowloon, Hong Kong is in a resettlement area. At present, living conditions are certainly better than they were in the original dwellings, but already they are overcrowded and dirty and conditions will get worse as more children are born. Outside the flats is a street market.

Top left : Although some fish are farmed by
rearing the young in tanks and releasing them later
into lagoons, oceanic fish farming is not yet
practicable on a large scale. Fish provide only two
per cent of world food. Centre : Molluscs are staple
food in parts of S.E. Asia, but as they rot quickly,
they are difficult to market economically. Top
right : Algae, once thought to have good potential
as food, need expensive processing. There is, however, much research being done into farming the sea.

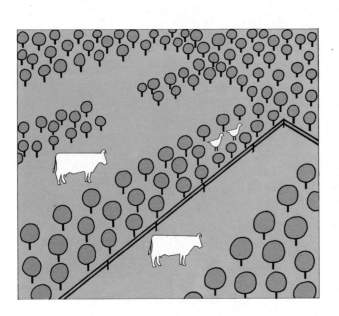

Above left : 3D-farming, brings tropical marginal
land into use. Tree legumes in rows provide shade ;
their roots contain bacteria that return nitrates to
the soil. Their fruit is cropped ; chickens eat
windfalls. Livestock graze on controlled pasture
between trees ; their manure acts as a fertilizer,
increasing pasture yields. The system is stable and
self-perpetuating. Above right : Eland antelopes
with cattle on a farm in Rhodesia. Game animals
do better than domesticated breeds on poor land.

Above: A selection or different legumes that are used as foods. Their importance is partly in their high protein content (p.172). Below: "Incaparina," a meal synthesized from maize, sorghum and cotton-seed; it is marketed in Central America. "Pronutro" is another, made from soya, groundnuts and fish.

Right: Tremendous strides are being made in conventional agriculture. This is a typical factory farm of the type needed if the world's people are to be fed. New cereals too are revolutionizing agriculture in the developing countries (p.171).

Eat Now Pay Later Meanwhile—ironically—we must produce more, cheaper, and better food, to feed more and more people. There are certain internationally orientated bodies that do research on methods of improving food production all over the world. Perhaps the best-known of these is the Food and Agriculture Organization (FAO), with its headquarters in Rome. It is a department of the United Nations that exists to give advice and technical assistance to the developing countries on techniques of food production and harvesting. The FAO and other similar bodies sponsor research on new strains of food crops, and on more efficient fertilizers and pesticides. Fertilizer factories and irrigation and drainage schemes are vital to any large-scale improvements in agriculture because any increased crop yield implies a greater drain on soil fertility.

Experience in Mexico and Israel has shown that tremendous improvements can be achieved by a planned and integrated programme; agriculture has formed the basis for more general economic expansion. But in much of the rest of the developing world, there is an ever-increasing backlog of hunger to make up, and increases in food production that merely keep up with the population rise are not enough. If there is to be a net gain, progress must be very much faster than ever before, and must be sustained over a long period. There is still vast room for progress—not only in conventional agriculture, but in farming technology, marketing, and storage. There is room for imagination, too; there are certainly many ways, some as yet unthought of, to provide new kinds of food—if people can only be persuaded to change their eating habits. Tastes in food, as in everything else, are largely the results of conditioning and tradition. Although traditions must be treated with respect, it is clear that, as food shortage becomes more and more acute, people will have to eat foods that they have never eaten before (p. 168–9).

Much of the world outside North America is still dependent for its grain on U.S. exports, but within a few years she too will cease to be an exporter, because her own increase of population will absorb all the surplus. When this

Left: A genetics and plant breeding laboratory where scientists work on producing improved rice strains by irradiation. Research using new and sophisticated techniques is replacing the more traditional methods of producing hybrids by crossing. Right: Dwarf hybrids —wheat in this case—stand up to the wind and rain much better than the long stemmed variety (on the left of the picture), which have lodged because their stalks are too slender. Lodging causes tremendous losses in cereal yields.

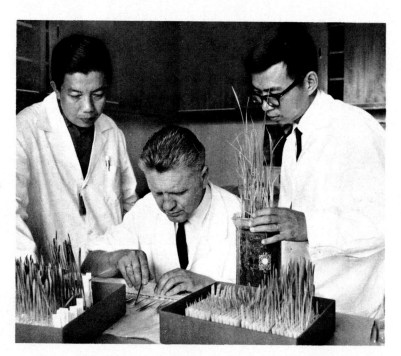

happens every nation will *have* to become self-supporting. This will be a good thing in certain ways because foreign aid has harmful side-effects. It forces local prices down and thereby reduces farmers' incentive to increase their own production. (On the arrival of food aid in the Congo, for instance, many farmers temporarily stopped chicken farming.) It is fundamental conservation policy to stimulate people to help themselves; increased production must rely on local labour and, if possible, on local resources; in short, food must be produced where the mouths are. However, the results of long and highly financed agricultural research can initiate a programme of self-help from outside, and the research that is resulting in one of the world's greatest food revolutions is a very fine example of international co-operation.

Dwarf Cereals   The Norin gene for dwarfing in wheat was discovered in Japan shortly after World War II. In 1962 the India Agricultural Research Institute IARI) realized its importance. A year later, the Rockefeller Foundation transferred into India several new strains bred and tried out in Mexico and the U.S.A. with great success.

There are at least two important hybrid strains; one of them, *sonora 64*, with a protein content of 14 per cent (against the usual average of 12 per cent), can be irradiated with gamma rays to produce another strain, *sharbati sonora*, with a protein content of as much as 16·5 per cent, and this strain gives 2·8 tons per acre—a very high yield indeed. In each of the 17 states of India, one area has been included in a special Intensive Agricultural Districts Programme. In these districts a training and education programme has been introduced simultaneously with the new hybrid cereal, as well as price assurance for the farmer and arrangements for co-operative marketing. The yield barrier has certainly been broken, and the value of farm produce has increased about six-fold in 1966–7. But fertilizer consumption has also increased almost eight-fold during the period from 1960–7, because any increase in a crop means a corresponding drain on soil nutrients.

Asia has always produced (and consumed) most of its own rice; and in response to ever-increasing demand, the International Rice Institute at Manila in the Philippines, with the co-operation of the Ford Foundation, produced a new strain called IR8 or, more familiarly, "Miracle Rice." It is just over 3 ft. high (developed from an original strain about 5 ft. high), and is resistant to disease, heavy winds, and monsoon rains. Japan too has made a tremendous breakthrough; using gamma rays from Cobalt-60 to irradiate rice fields, a strain with twice the original protein content has been developed.

Protein from Plants   Adults require about 50 gm. of protein a day to keep healthy. There are about 22 amino acids that combine to form the different proteins, and our bodies need a daily supply of 8 specific ones. Meat, fish, eggs, and dairy products contain all the necessary amino acids, but if these sources of animal protein are not available in sufficient quantities (and to about two thirds of the world's population they definitely are not), then vegetable proteins must be substituted.

Despite their increased protein content, the new cereals alone do not provide a balanced diet; neither do they contain all the necessary amino acids, nor do they contain them in the quantity necessary for health, growth, and cell replacement. But these can be supplemented by food from other protein-rich crops. The main protein-rich crops are oilseeds and legumes. The principle oilseeds are soybeans, groundnuts, sunflower seeds, cotton seeds, sesame, and coconuts. Unfortunately all except the last two contain toxins that must be removed by processing, and this increases the cost of production. Groundnuts, for instance, must be fumigated in the field with ammonia and phosphine to eliminate the mould that produces the toxin. The crop can then be gathered and compounded with other nutrients into a meal (p.169). Oilseeds must be supplemented with legumes (also known as *pulse crops*) in order to achieve a balanced complement of amino acids. Grain legumes (such as broad beans, chickpeas, and lentils) and tree legumes (for instance, alga-roba and carob trees) are grown as crops in a number of developing countries. The advantage of legumes is that they provide their own nitrogenous fertilizer. Tree legumes have an extra advantage in that they can reach groundwater at very deep levels with their long tap-roots. It is therefore no accident that many tropical trees are legumes, and these facts point the way to extended use of such trees in dry climates where the soil is infertile. Some experts believe that, if fully exploited, oilseed and legume proteins could meet almost the entire present (if not the future) world protein deficit.

Meat is Wasteful   We saw in Chapter 2 how the food chain is made up of primary producers (plants) and of the consumers that depend on them, either directly or at second hand. There is a 90-per-cent energy loss in the conversion of plant food into animal protein; thus the more we "cream the top off" the food chain, the more we are wasting the energy that was originally provided

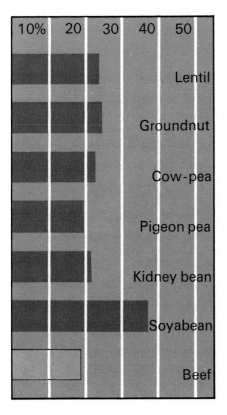

Above: Comparison of the protein content in various legumes and in beef. Carbohydrate content is almost as high as in cereals (about 60 per cent) and fat is low except in soya and groundnuts.

Above: After the saiga was hunted to near extinction, the Russians bred it in reserves, restocked marginal land and now crop it for meat with great success. Below left: Wildebeeste, farmed on savannah. Right: The capybara; not yet farmed but possibly a very practical new protein source.

by primary producers. If we could find a way to convert something from further down the chain, such as marine plankton, into a cheap and palatable protein, it would be far better conservation policy than to eat meat (from primary consumers) and fish (which are almost always secondary consumers).

Eating meat is also wasteful of land if the land on which we graze animals could be used for growing food crops. So it becomes good conservation policy to farm animals on marginal land that is no good for high-yield cultivation. Domesticated cattle, which thrive on Europe's temperate grasslands, do not do well on marginal land in the tropics. Accordingly it has been found worth while to use some of it for farming wild game. These animals are far more economical of pasture and water, and they also give meat of high quality. They have an added advantage in that they are already immune to many endemic diseases that cause havoc among imported cattle. Apart from the eland antelope (p. 168) other wild animals that are being farmed include the wildebeeste, and the Russian saiga antelope. A large South American rodent, the capybara, has been suggested too, and ecologically it is in some ways a winner, because it feeds on aquatic vegetation and therefore does not compete for pasture with truly terrestrial animals.

Certain golden rules of land use are beginning to become clearer now. For instance, if a single species of game is grazed over a particular area it may eat itself out of pasture. But by applying ecological principles the pasture can be kept in good condition indefinitely. This can be done by grazing several types of animal over a single area (provided that the different species do not eat the same plants), thus simulating natural conditions more closely. By contrast, the practice of growing a single crop over a vast area (*monoculture*) is ecologically dangerous even though it has to be done because high yields are needed. This is because monoculture calls for the cutting back of the normal climax community. Vital components of the ecosystem, such as weeds that support a local insect fauna, form a natural guard against invading pests. Without them, the crop is very vulnerable to pests, and this in turn calls for careful use of pesticides (p. 178).

This is why conservationists consider multiple land use such as 3D forestry (p. 168) as wise use of land. It gives a good self-perpetuating food yield that is optimum for that type of marginal land. It is not the true climax for the area, but it comes very close to being a stable, though artificial, ecosystem, in which enough of the essential components are present to combat pests and to keep the soil as fertile as possible.

As only two fifths of the land surface of the earth is arable or even marginal land, what is the general attitude of conservationists toward the rest? One fifth is permanent ice and snow, another fifth is desert, and the remaining fifth is mountainous or covered in primeval forest.

The first priority is to stabilize desert sands and prevent them encroaching on surrounding good land, either by spraying them with petroleum mulch or by planting them with marram grass or even a fodder crop. Once they have been partly stabilized they can be used for animal pasture, and so eventually

Right: Preventing soil erosion in Ceylon by terracing. Other ways include planting shelter belts, and contour ploughing. This uses the natural curvature of the land and prevents water from running down the slopes in ever deepening gulleys.

a soil may build up. As regards mountains, it is impractical to consider mountain slopes as high-potential agricultural land. The soils are usually absent or poor; and cultivation requires the land to be terraced, but agricultural machinery cannot be used on narrow ledges. Yet it is surprising how many people have, throughout history, eked out their living by terrace farming. As a means of controlling erosion, terraces are efficient, but constructing them is costly in time and labour. Afforestation not only prevents erosion but can provide a timber or fodder crop as well. Here, too, a soil can eventually be built up so that the forest becomes self-perpetuating.

This brings us to one of the biggest hazards of land conservation—misleading appearances. Nearly half the forested area of the earth is covered by tropical rain-forests. These have an appearance that seems to be the quintessence of fertility. Below the rich and luxuriant growth of trees and creepers, the topsoil is brown and deep. Too many farmers have believed this soil to be worth farming and have felled great areas of rain-forest and planted

crops. Disaster always follows: the first heavy rain washes away the topsoil and the crop with it. The floodwater, laden with silt, blocks rivers and buries farmland miles away. Then, between rainstorms, the ground dries out and sets rock hard, and soil micro-organisms are killed by the heat of direct exposure to the sun. This residual soil, an aluminium-rich *laterite*, is quite useless for cultivation. It acts, in the complex of the rain-forest, as a very transitory staging post for the salts that are produced when vegetation rots (and in that humid heat, it rots very quickly). Normally the valuable nutrients are quickly absorbed by other vegetation. Thus, luxuriant forest growth is deceptive; it is like a shop window in which all the stock is displayed and nothing is held in reserve. In this case, conservation means leaving the forest alone, however great the need for agricultural or any other type of productive land may be.

Fuel and Power   If we were to rely on solar energy for all our energy needs we should have to be content with an agrarian economy and just about enough power to cook, to warm the house, and to heat the bath water—and this only in sunny regions. We are, however, used to much more than this; our civilization and the things that go with it—industry, transport, consumer goods, heating, lighting—all depend on energy from sources other than photosynthesis. Up till now, our extra energy has mostly been derived from falling water, from burning fossil fuels—coal, oil, and gas—and recently from atomic fission of a radio-active isotope of uranium. None of these energy resources is in infinite supply, but they are adequate for some time to come.

But energy resources are unequally distributed in the world, and without energy the underdeveloped countries cannot industrialize—and industrialize they must, if they are to be self-supporting. Foreign investment has helped in some countries, but not where the problem is most acute. We are forced to think again of India: who is going to continue to invest in India when the hundreds of millions of dollars worth of aid already poured in by the U.S.A. and the World Bank merely gets engulfed in a bottomless pit. Two things are becoming increasingly clear; the first is that these debts will never be repaid; the second is that the World Bank, in which the United States is a dominant force, knows very well what the situation is, but has adopted a policy of periodic injections of aid, primarily to keep social unrest from boiling over and to prevent India from going Communist. And, what is more, their motives are well understood by many officials in the Indian government, who therefore bitterly resent this aid. To say that the rich should give to the poor may be good conservation theory, but it is naive and unrealistic. As long as strings are attached to investment or aid, developing countries cannot acquire the energy they need without becoming pawns in power politics.

Right: Maps of the distribution of a few of the world's more important non-renewable resources show, for instance, that the Northern Hemisphere is far richer than the Southern in energy resources. This could be balanced if deuterium (centre) of which there are infinite quantities in the sea, could be harnessed. New deposits of metal ores and oil are continually being discovered. The problem is not one of overall shortage but of maldistribution, and stock-piling of surpluses.

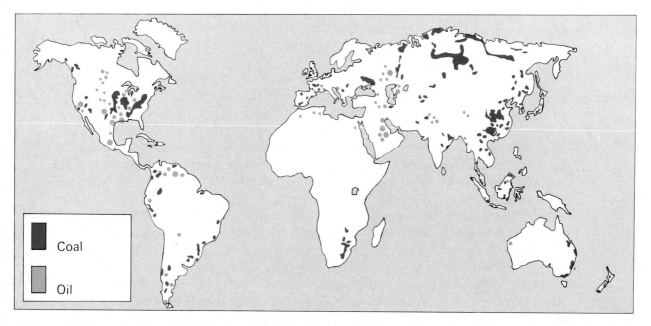

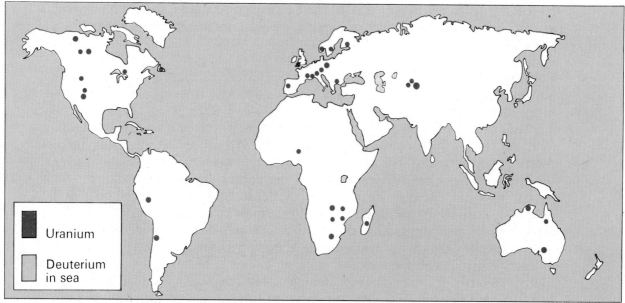

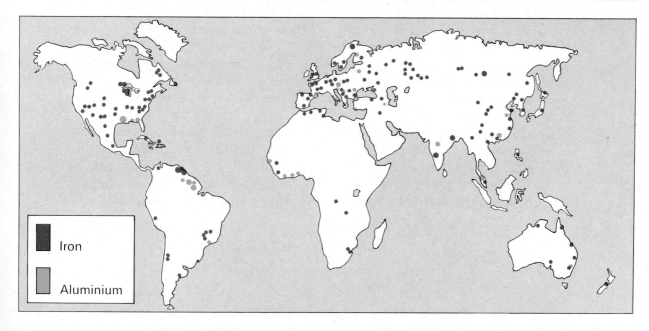

There is also another, quite different, aspect of the energy problem. The combustion of fossil fuels over the past century has resulted in an increase of almost 14 per cent in the carbon dioxide content of the atmosphere. This carbon dioxide lets sunlight in but prevents heat from escaping into space; the earth is becoming like a huge greenhouse. The overall temperature of the earth is being raised and some experts think that the Antarctic and Greenland ice-caps will melt within 400 years (others put the figure at more like 4000 years). At all events, it would not take much melting to raise the level of the sea sufficiently to drown much of the world's inhabited land. It is unlikely that fossil fuels will for this reason cease to be used, especially as atomic power is still expensive to produce, and is of no use for cars or aeroplanes, which need fuel they can carry about with them.

There is however an additional power source—heavy hydrogen or deuterium, present in the oceans in such quantities that if harnessed as *fusion power* it would provide an ample supply of power for millions of years. Research into fusion power, still in the experimental stages, should be treated as a priority; if the ice-caps start to melt, we may not have as long a breathing space as we think.

Fouling our Nest We in the industrial societies may have certain comforts not shared by the rest of the world, but we are also in some danger of polluting this planet and making it uninhabitable. Pollution—a by-product of our civilization—has two main sources. The first is the unleashing of chemicals and rubbish onto nature in such *forms* that nature cannot break them down. The second is by releasing relatively harmless substances onto a healthy ecosystem in such *quantities* that they upset the natural balance.

Into the first category come toxic pesticides, radio-active fall-out, and certain industrial by-products. Pesticides such as dieldrin and DDT, for instance, are persistent, and the residue—though harmless in its original concentration—builds up inside living things, becoming more concentrated at each stage in the food chain, until it becomes lethal. Into the second category comes domestic sewage, which is broken down successfully in the highly aerated waters of rivers, but only until the concentration becomes too high. Nitrates in fertilizers are harmless until they percolate from the fields via rivers into lakes. Then they stimulate toxic algae to such vigorous growth that all other life in the lake is killed. Also, residual nitrate in drinking water is poisonous, especially to babies. Today sewage and industrial effluent are threatening to overwhelm even Lake Baikal, the deepest lake in the world and the store of one fifth of all freshwater reserves; and most of Lake Erie is already dead.

Gradually, as more research is being done, the short- and long-term effects of pollution are becoming better understood. One thing clearly emerges; most waste is not indisposable and most air and water pollution can be prevented, or at any rate reduced. In the U.S.A. and Canada, there is already severe legislation compelling townships and industries to clean up their effluent before dumping it. It is a straightforward affair to cleanse smoke of toxic gases before it leaves the factory chimney, to burn all possible combustible waste, to use only nontoxic pesticides, and to be very much more stringent about the disposal of radio-active waste from atomic power stations. Pollution control may be expensive, but it is surely a top priority. Once the damage is done it is often irreversible; we cannot afford to make another bucketful of fresh water stagnant and stinking, nor to turn one square inch more of our earth into a wasteland.

The gradual change of emphasis in this book is not accidental. It follows, in a sense, a historical path, reflecting the attitudes of conservationists through the last 200 years or so. We began with those early days when conservation was about providing places for people to sport and for wildlife to live unmolested. Gradually we have seen how the priorities have changed; and if there are still conservationists who can make global generalization about saving the Earth from ruin by human beings we know now that they are speaking of fantasy, not fact.

We should look at the world as we would at a huge and infinitely detailed jigsaw puzzle in which the pieces are lying jumbled together in a heap and the picture of how it should look is not very clear. But gradually we fit in a piece here and a piece there. This may not seem much after the hopes we cherished; but grandiose and unrealistic dreams lead to cynicism and a kind of impotence in which nothing gets done at all. The prospect of having to correct the mistakes of centuries is rather overpowering, though the need for action is plain enough.

The main burden of reparation must fall on specialists, teachers, farmers, town planners, doctors, industrialists, and sociologists; but it is up to each and every one of us, and particularly the parents of the next generation, to love the world and treat it with respect—and to try to fit in a piece of that jigsaw puzzle.

This is a post-script; not in the mainstream of conservation, but important all the same. We live in a society in which machines and industry are, and will continue to be, part of our lives. At the start of this book we talked of changes in attitudes towards Nature as men sought its beauty in new ways. Our medium is industry and we must seek its own particular beauty or live poorer lives. The young sculptor, who made this piece from industrial debris, is aware, as are countless others like him, that this medium expresses something of immediacy that could bring us into closer harmony with what still seems a bleak and hostile environment.

INDEX

Page numbers in *italics* refer to illustrations or captions to illustrations.

ACKNOWLEDGMENTS

Key to position of picture on page: (B) bottom, (C) centre, (L) left, (R) right, (T) top; hence (BR) bottom right, (CL) centre left, etc.

Endpapers ATP Bilderdienst Zürich

Title George Evans/ Camera Press

10 & 13 (T) Reproduced by permission of the Trustees of the British Museum

13 (B) Uni-Dia-Verlag, Stuttgart

15 Radio Times Hulton Picture Library

16 Photo John Freeman © Aldus Books/ Reproduced by courtesy of the Trustees, The National Gallery, London

17 Photo John Webb © Aldus Books/ Courtesy The Tate Gallery, London

19 Concord Free Public Library

21 (T) Photo J. Allan Cash (B) Photo Edward Poulton © Aldus Books

22 Jane Burton/Bruce Coleman Ltd.

24 (TL) Photo L. K. Shumway (BL) after Arthur W. Calston, *The Life of the Green Plant*, © 1961. By permission of Prentice-Hall, Inc., Englewood Cliffs, New Jersey.

25 Zentrale Farbbild Agentur Düsseldorf

27 Donald Patterson/ Bruce Coleman Ltd.

28 H. M. B. Barnfather/ Bruce Coleman Ltd.

29 (TL) (B) Dr. W. B. Kendrick, Department of Biology, University of Waterloo, Ontario

30
31 Popperfoto
33 Chuck Abbott/Rapho Guillumette Pictures

36 (T) Solarfilma S.F., Reykjavik (B) & 37 Photos Dennis Brokaw, San Diego

39 (T) Leonard Lee Rue III/Bruce Coleman Ltd. (B) Wisconsin Conservation Department of Natural Resources

40 Mansell Collection
43 (TL) Photo by courtesy of the B.B.C. (TR) Radio Times Hulton Picture Library (B) Aldus Archives

45 (T) Photo Geoffrey Drury © Aldus Books (B) Des Bartlett/Bruce Coleman Ltd.

46 American Geographical Society

47 (B) Joe Van Wormer/ Bruce Coleman Ltd.

48 George E. Hyde, F.R.E.S.

49 United States Information Service, London

52 (T) Photo United States Department of Agriculture (B) & 53 (B) Brookhaven National Laboratory

53 (T) Photo Geoffrey Kinns at the British Museum (Natural History)

55 Imperial War Museum, London

56 Tierbilder Okapia, Frankfurt/Main

59 (T) Reproduced by permission of the Trustees of the British Museum (B) Sven Gillsater/ Bruce Coleman Ltd.

61 Painting by George A. Catlin, Courtesy of The American Museum of Natural History

62 The Bettmann Archive
63 after drawing by Otto Van Ersel

64 George Holton/Bruce Coleman Ltd.

65 Jane Burton/Bruce Coleman Ltd.

68 (T) R. T. Peterson/ Bruce Coleman Ltd.

68–69 (B) British Museum (Natural History)

69 (TL) Christian Zuber/ World Wildlife Fund (TR) Photo Peter Poole © Aldus Books

72—73 (T) Zentrale Farbbild Agentur Düsseldorf

72 (BL) Bruce Coleman Ltd.

73 (B) James Simon/ Bruce Coleman Ltd.

74 (T) & 75 Radio Times Hulton Picture Library (B) Richard Harrington/ Camera Press

79 Klaus Gottfredsen
80 (L) Joe Van Wormer/ Bruce Coleman Ltd.

81 (T) & (B) Photos Edward S. Ross

83 Tierbilder Okapia, Frankfurt/Main

84 (L) Popperfoto (R) Photo Harry Frauca

85 (T) Jan MacPhail/ Bruce Coleman Ltd. (B) Photos Robert Cundy

88 Jane Burton/Bruce Coleman Ltd.

90 (L) Mary Evans Picture Library (R) British Crown Copyright

91 London Express
93 (T) Photo Kevin Carver © Aldus Books (B) Photo T. Dennett

96 (T) Graham M. Pizzey/ Bruce Coleman Ltd. (B) Jane Burton/Bruce

Coleman Ltd.

97 Photo The Phoenix Zoo

98 (L) French Government Tourist Office, London (R) Tierpark Hellabrunn, München/ Photo Toni Angermayer

99 Tierbilder Okapia, Frankfurt/Main

100 (L) Popperfoto (R) Picturepoint, London

101 (T) Zentrale Farbbild Agentur Düsseldorf (B) Tierpark Hellabrunn, München/ Photo Toni Angermayer

104 (L) & 105 (R) Photos San Diego Zoo (R) Tierbilder Okapia, Frankfurt/Main

105 (L) Budapest Zoo/ Photo Gyorgy Kapocsy

106 Thor Larsen/World Wildlife Fund

108 (L) Photo D. A. Ratcliffe (R) Zentrale Farbbild Agentur Düsseldorf

109 Picturepoint, London

112 (L) Sally Anne Thompson/Animal Photography (R) Zentrale Farbbild Agentur Düsseldorf

113 Picturepoint, London

116 (T) (BL) Photos Bill Cowen, Keswick (BR) Des Bartlett/Bruce Coleman Ltd.

117 (T) (CR) Photos Bill Cowen, Keswick (TL) South African National Parks Board (BL) Hans Schmied/ Bavaria, PAF International (BR) Des Bartlett/Bruce Coleman Ltd.

118 Mel Ruder/Camera Press

119 (T) Photo J. Allan Cash (B) Terence Spencer/

121 Camera Press Novosti Press Agency

124-125 Harrison Forman World Photos

126 Douglas Botting/ Camera Press

127-128, 129 (B) Photos Josef Muench, Santa Barbara

129 (T) Photo D. C. Williamson, London

131 (L) Photo Norman Myers, Nairobi (R) Photo J. Allan Cash

132 Japan National Tourist Organization, London

133 Harrison Forman World Photos

134 Photos Josef Muench, Santa Barbara

136-137 Photo Kevin Carver© Aldus Books

138 Photo Stuart Stevens © Aldus Books

140-141 Based on a map by George Philip & Son Ltd.

143 Photo The Wellcome Museum, London

148 (B) after W. and P. Paddock, Famine 1975, Weidenfeld & Nicholson Ltd., London

148 (T) & 149 after ed. Philip M. Hauser The Population Dilemma, © 1963 by The American Assembly, Columbia University, New York. Prentice-Hall, Inc., Englewood Cliffs, New Jersey

151 (TL) Photo Jean Vertut (TR) Photo J. Allan Cash (B) Paul Almasy

152 (TL) (BL) International Planned Parenthood Federation, London

152-153 (C) & 153 (TR) Asociacion Chilena de Proteccion de le Familia, Santiago

153 (BR) Photo Bernard Cole/Planned Parenthood Federation of America

157 (B) after Bernard Berelson and Ronald Freedman, A Study in Fertility Control. © May 1964, Scientific American, Inc. All rights reserved

160 (L) Harrison Forman World Photos

161 & 163 Paul Almasy

164 John Launois/Black Star Publishing Co. Inc., New York

167 Photo J. Allan Cash

168 (T), 169 (TR) (CR) Photos Stuart Stephenson

168-169 (CB) Des Bartlett/Bruce Coleman Ltd.

169 (TL) Douglas Wilson (BR) Photo Geoffrey Drury © Aldus Books

170 International Atomic Energy Agency, Vienna

171 The Rockfeller Foundation, New York

173 (TR) Photo Ken Coton © Aldus Books (BL) Simon Trevor/ Bruce Coleman Ltd. (BR) Russ Kinne/Bruce Coleman Ltd.

175 Paul Almasy/Camera Press

177 Based on information from The Faber Atlas, Faber and Faber Ltd., London

179 Photo David Litchfield/ © Aldus Books

ARTISTS' CREDITS

Rudolph Britto 24 (BL)

Maurice Sweeney 140-141, 145 (T) (B), 148 (T) (B), 149, 157 (B), 160 (R), 168 (BL), 173 (TL)

Graham Wall 29 (TR), 47 (T), 63